YOUR RETIREMENT GAME PLAN

YOUR RETIREMENT GAME PLAN

30+ YEARS OF CONFIDENCE: NO PENSION REQUIRED

SAM MARRELLA

LIONCREST
PUBLISHING

YOUR RETIREMENT GAME PLAN
30+ Years of Confidence: No Pension Required

ISBN 978-1-61961-763-6 *Paperback*
978-1-61961-764-3 *Ebook*

This book is dedicated to the very special people in my life.

First, to my mom and dad, Mary Jo and Paul A. Marrella, who gave me everything I ever needed and supported me every step of the way.

To my lovely wife, Sue, who has inspired me to be the best person I can possibly be. I can't thank her enough for her endless love and support.

And finally, to my children, Ashleigh and Sammy, who are truly the best kids I could possibly have asked for. You make me incredibly proud to be your father, each and every day.

CONTENTS

DISCLAIMER

IMPORTANT: The projections or other information generated by Goal Planning & Monitoring regarding the likelihood of various investment outcomes are hypothetical in nature, do not reflect actual investment results, and are not guarantees of future results. The return assumptions in Goal Planning & Monitoring are not reflective of any specific product, and do not include any fees or expenses that may be incurred by investing in specific products. The actual returns of a specific product may be more or less than the returns used in Goal Planning & Monitoring. It is not possible to directly invest in an index. Financial forecasts, rates of return, risk, inflation, and other assumptions may be used as the basis for illustrations. They should not be considered a guarantee of future performance or a guarantee of achieving overall financial objectives. Past performance is not a guarantee or a predictor of future results of either the indices or any particular investment. Goal Planning & Monitoring results may vary with each use and over time.

The information contained in this book does not purport to be a complete description of the securities, markets, or developments referred to in this material. The information has been obtained from sources considered to be reliable, but we do not guarantee that the foregoing material is accurate or complete. Any information is not a complete summary or statement of all available data necessary for making an investment decision and does not constitute a recommendation. Any opinions of the chapter authors are those of the chapter authors and not necessarily those of Raymond James Financial Services, Inc. or Raymond James. Expressions of opinion are as of the initial book publishing date and are subject to change without notice. Raymond James Financial Services, Inc. is not responsible for the consequences of any particular transaction or investment decision based on the content of this book. All financial, retirement, and estate planning should be individualized as each person's situation is unique. This information is not intended as a solicitation or an offer to buy or sell any security referred to herein. Keep in mind that there is no assurance that our recommendations or strategies will ultimately be successful or profitable, nor protect against a loss. There may also be the potential for missed growth opportunities that may occur after the sale of an investment. Recommendations, specific investments, or strategies discussed may not be suitable for all investors. Past performance may not be indicative of future results. You should discuss any tax or legal matters with the appropriate professional. Every investor's situation is unique and you should consider your investment goals, risk tolerance, and time horizon before making any investment. Investing involves risk and you may incur a profit or loss regardless of strategy selected.

INTRODUCTION

GETTING PAST THE FEAR FACTOR

A man ninety years old was asked to what he attributed his longevity. "I reckon," he said, with a twinkle in his eye, "it was because most nights I went to bed and slept when I should have sat up and worried."

—GARSON KANIN

Hardly anything in life scares people as much as their finances.

Hit by a winter blizzard? Turn up the heat and hunker down. Wandered into a scary neighborhood? Call a cab. Handed an unexpected medical diagnosis? Find a good doctor, take your meds, and get lots of rest.

But your money? Especially your *retirement* money? How can you possibly protect yourself there?

You know that playing it totally safe won't necessarily solve your problems, and might even create more. You don't trust your own planning, but you're afraid to let some slick salesman through your door. You've done a ton of online research and read a whole stack of books, but you've uncovered so much contradictory information that you find yourself back at square one, having done nothing at all.

Then there's the media. Every time you open a paper or a blog or tune in to CNBC, they tell you the world has moved a couple inches closer to the Apocalypse. In fact, it's coming any minute, so you better read this article *right now.* And you better make some fast moves with your money because the markets are about to get clobbered. Gold is about to skyrocket. A crisis in Asia will probably spread to New York. A crisis in New York will probably spread to Asia. "Volatility on Wall Street" is probably the most common headline I know.

As a wealth manager, I hear from my clients that fear often steals the fun out of the word "retirement." Really. Fear can suck the joy out of the whole deal. It turns out that fishing just isn't the same if you're checking the finance app on your iPhone as you leave the dock.

Now, retirement didn't always equal fear. Housing and healthcare didn't always cost so much, and people didn't live as long. Plus, once upon a time, lots of people had a nice thing called a "pension" that brought certainty and stability to their later years. But few of us have pensions anymore, and even those of us who do often find those checks inadequate to fuel the fun we imagined having. You know—the fun that's meant to start the day after that last day at the office.

If you've been smart and diligent, you've probably saved up a nest egg for retirement. And pension or no pension, you're probably wondering how the heck to make it last thirty-plus years. Maybe you're trying to figure out whether you're in a position to retire. Maybe you're trying to decide how to divide up your money between the market and safer alternatives. Maybe you're not so happy to hear that retirees today could easily live to the age of 103, or older.

If any of the above describes your situation, this little book is for you. Why?

Because my goal is to take the fear out of retiring, with or without a pension.

This book lays out a simple strategy to turn whatever nest egg you have accumulated into a long-term, multi-stage income generator that addresses the three great risks of retirement. Let's start by looking those risks straight in the eye.

- Risk #1: Timing. Retiring before you're ready or right before a downturn in the markets.
- Risk #2: Inflation. Having your money lose purchasing power over time.
- Risk #3: Longevity. Living longer than you can afford.

There you go. We made a start, right? Even breaking out our fears into specific categories gives us some power over them.

Your Retirement Game Plan lays out a simple, mathematically sound, real-life-tested method for making your nest egg generate sufficient income, divided into discrete segments of time, to take you all the way through your retirement years. Executed properly and consistently, this game plan can drop the three great risks nearly to zero.

Seriously. Even in the twenty-first century. And even if you have no pension.

The game plan is not complicated and it is not magic. Simply put, if you stay the course, it will give you a high probability of not outliving your money while enjoying the lifestyle you enjoy.

How much of a nest egg will you need in order to make your game plan work? Well, I had to pick a minimum to create models with an appropriate outcome. So, you will find this book geared toward folks who don't have a pension or other dependable income streams beyond Social Security, but who will have accumulated at least $1 million in 2017 dollars before they plan to fully retire.

If you aren't quite there yet, you should still read this book. First, it may help you better time your retirement. Second, the game plan can be used with *any* size nest egg to create a reliable income stream for thirty-plus years. Your lifestyle may be just fine with less income, and you may find another way to supplement your income when you retire from full-time work.

THE FOURTH GREAT RISK

"With confidence, you have won before you have started."

—MARCUS GARVEY

I started out by talking about fear because I think it's not just an emotional spoiler for retirement, but a financial spoiler as well. In fact, I call it the fourth great risk.

- Risk #4: Fear. When you retire, the fear factors generated by our society may cause you to make really bad financial decisions.

When people go from earning a paycheck to living off their portfolio, they often encounter a whole new kind of fear: loss of control. They worry they no longer have personal leverage over their monetary well-being. They feel they're suddenly living at the mercy of Wall Street or the Hang Sheng Index.

Often, this uncertainty causes them to behave badly financially. It's understandable, because most folks have not been trained to smile through the roller coaster of markets. They never had to learn the emotional skills necessary for good investing because they were cultivating other skills—like earning a living. Before retirement, when their 401(k) fund went down, they continued to contribute money and knew they did not need that money until sometime in the future. This knowledge provided the emotional base and stability they needed.

But now that retirement has come, the future is now. And now (as always), the media is doing its best to scare them. In fact, come retirement, folks have even more time to listen to CNBC and read financial blogs. When the markets rise, they find it easy to resist the doomsayers. But when the markets get rocked, people start listening to the rhetoric. It's loud. It's everywhere. And then they make mistakes. Often those mistakes include things like panic selling all their stocks during a big market drop and going completely to cash.

It's painful to watch your accounts and portfolio income go down. Especially now that you are no longer receiving a paycheck. Already that's a big change, so watching your portfolio fall feels like a tackle and a pile on. You want to stop the pain immediately—but stopping your pain temporarily may be the exact wrong thing to do.

Every day, I help people plan for the first three great risks of retirement. But my most important job may be helping them avoid that fourth great risk. In fact, some of the proudest moments in my long career as a wealth manager have been teaching people to weather trying times without succumbing to fear.

How do you escape Risk #4: Fear? By creating a strategic game plan and sticking with it. By recognizing that pain and adversity *are part of any game,* including retirement.

You will hear a lot of sports metaphors in this book. That's no coincidence. I believe that sports, especially team sports, provide great emotional preparation for the bigger games in life. My own youth was shaped by basketball, and

I plan on telling you a couple of stories from my basketball days to show you what I'm talking about.

For now, I want to say that in sports, as in life, it's crucial not to get blinded by emotions. Not to get "psyched out." It's also crucial to work with your team and not assume you have to face every challenge on your own. Much of my personal satisfaction has come from being part of my client's "team." As a wealth manager, I help my clients look at their whole life situation and then use that information to help them make good decisions with their money. I enjoy nothing more than working with folks to create their own personal game plan, and then to figure out how to retire confidently, regardless of conditions on the playing field.

I tell clients, "I don't want you to go into retirement worried about the Dow.[1] I don't want you to lose sleep over oil prices. I want you to go into retirement wondering what great things you will do with your grandkids. What trips you will take. Who and what you will have time to get to know better."

---

1 The Dow Jones Industrial Average (DJIA), commonly known as "The Dow," is an index representing thirty stocks of companies maintained and reviewed by the editors of the *Wall Street Journal*. Inclusion of these indexes is for illustrative purposes only. Keep in mind that individuals cannot invest directly in any index, and index performance does not include transaction costs or other fees, which will affect actual investment performance. Individual investor's results will vary. Past performance does not guarantee future results.

That's what retirement's all about. It's not about being stressed out over your investments. But unless you create confidence in not just your retirement *nest egg,* but your retirement *income,* you can't really enjoy what could well be the best years of your life.

ALL ROADS MUST LEAD TO INCOME

"I'm going to retire and live off my savings. What I'll do the second day, I have no idea."

—ANONYMOUS

Prospective clients ask me all the time, "Sam, how much of a nest egg do I need in order to retire comfortably?"

My answer usually consists of three words: "It all depends."

It all depends, I say, because I don't know enough about you. I don't know enough about your financial situation, your lifestyle, your family, your goals and dreams. What does your Social Security look like? Did your spouse work? Do they have Social Security or are they going to opt for Spousal Social Security, which is basically half of yours? Do you have any debt?

Then I tell them they've started by asking the wrong question altogether.

"You see, it's really not about your nest egg. *It's about your income.*" The first question people should ask themselves is not "how much money do I need," but "how much income do I need, and where is it going to come from?"

And just as importantly, how will I make that income *grow* over time?

Financial independence does not come from eating through a pile of money; it comes from investing money to create future income streams. When we put money into a 401(k), we don't put it there so it grows to $1 million...and then proceed to spend that million dollars when we retire. *We need that million dollars to create an income stream that helps to replace the paycheck we no longer receive.*

I tell them, "All financial roads must lead to income. If they don't, you may have made some wrong turns."

And the importance of income *growth?* If you are going to live thirty-plus years, *you know* that inflation will be your enemy. So you have to create an income stream that doesn't just continue, but *gets larger over time.* Otherwise, it's unlikely you'll be able to maintain your standard of living throughout retirement.

I've got to tell you that most people don't consider inflation.

They smile and say, "I'm retired today, and today I need this much income!" When I ask them about inflation and longevity—about their situation twenty to twenty-five years in the future—they look at me like I'm some kind of monster who has come to destroy their dreams.

That's when I have to step them through an indisputable truth of history: Costs have *always* increased. I ask them to consider how much things cost today versus ten, fifteen, and twenty years ago. Are they aware, for example, that Motel 6 got its name because when it opened it charged just six dollars a night? Inflation is real. There's just no avoiding the issue.

Once again, I am not trying to instill fear, I am trying to prompt logical planning. I like to put it this way:

Living a long life is not a bad thing. It's just really expensive.

TIMING MAY NOT BE EVERYTHING, BUT...

"I learned that we can do anything, but we can't do everything... at least not at the same time. So think of your priorities not in terms of what activities you do, but when you do them. Timing is everything."

—DAN MILLMAN

When people ask me if they have enough of a nest egg to retire, they're not thinking about *income*. They're not thinking about *inflation*. And just as importantly, they are not thinking about Risk #1: Timing.

One of the biggest retirement planning decisions you will make is exactly when to retire. We will discuss the details of timing your retirement later on. For now, let me just say that I've seen plenty of mistakes over three decades of helping people manage their wealth—and too often, those mistakes come from retiring too early.

Once you officially retire, it's hard to make a comeback. If you retire for ten years and then decide you can't afford retirement and try to jump back into the workforce, you may find it pretty rough sledding.

No doubt, some people can return successfully after many years out of their field of expertise. But the world now changes so rapidly and technology progresses so swiftly that "unretiring" has become far more difficult than it was for our forebears. If you haven't actively kept up with the changes in your profession, just think how much less valuable you will be to potential employers. Think how much harder it will be to talk anyone into hiring you at age sixty-five or seventy or beyond. Chat with some of the older folks working as greeters at Walmart, and find out what career they retired from years ago.

When my clients do decide to retire, I want them to wake up not just the next day, but every day with confidence and peace of mind. When we sit down and complete their discovery meeting (see Chapter 3: The Wealth Management Consultative Process), it's not my job to tell them what they want to hear. It's my job to give them a professional opinion based on my more than thirty years in the business.

Sometimes I say flat out, "You cannot afford to retire right now, and here's why."

When I deliver this news, some people get angry and walk away. Even though I kiddingly ask them not to shoot the messenger, they, in essence, do just that. Sometimes I will decide not to engage them as clients because I don't see a good outcome from the decision they are so eager to make...and I don't feel I can make a difference in that outcome.

Most people would like every day to be a Saturday, but not everyone can afford every day to be a Saturday.

Even though you may be able to afford a lifestyle where

every day is a Saturday in the first year you retire, that doesn't mean you will be able to afford it five or ten years down the road.

My brother and business partner, Paul, claims, "The best dentists are those whose patients die with teeth in their mouths." I'm sure you could find a lot of other metrics on which to judge dentists, but that one's hard to argue with. In our world, the best wealth managers are those whose clients die with their bucket lists complete, smiles on their faces, and money still in their accounts. For us, it means job satisfaction. For our clients, it means their peace of mind.

TO RETIRE OR NOT TO RETIRE

"Most people don't plan to fail, they fail to plan."

—JOHN L. BECKLEY

Let me tell you about a client I'll call Bill.

Bill was sixty years old when we first met. One sunny morning, he showed up at my office, sat down with a happy glow, and told me that he "didn't need to do a lot of financial planning." He just wanted me to help him invest the 401(k) money he wanted to roll over. Seems he'd heard good things about me from his retired friends, and he'd seen one of my presentations at his office.

Bill was a middle manager at a big oil company, and a whole group of his colleagues were retiring just then. They had inspired him to take the plunge, too. Would I handle his retirement investments the way I was handling theirs?

It was great to hear about the votes of confidence from his colleagues. But I couldn't just dive into his investment options.

"If you don't mind, Bill," I said. "Before we get to your 401(k), maybe you could tell me a little about your personal situation."

He told me the size of his total nest egg, which was about $500,000, plus some assorted stocks. He told me about his Social Security and pension expectations. I learned that he still had a mortgage to pay off. He had a daughter who was a junior in high school and was just then applying to college.

When he added that his wife was only fifty-eight and not working, a cloud started to pass across my mind. Her age mattered to me a lot more than you might think. When you're husband and wife, you have to create a secure path into retirement for the both of you. In terms of longevity planning, I immediately began to look at both of them as fifty-eight, not sixty.

Bill hadn't thought through any kind of thirty-year plan—much less longer. He hadn't considered inflation. And he hadn't really thought about how to pay for his daughter's college expenses.

"When are you planning to retire, Bill?" I asked gently.

"I just did! They had a retirement party for me on Saturday. I am now a free man. Well, technically I'm not officially retired until I use up a few vacation days I have left. But I stopped going into the office as of Monday morning! Now that I'm retired, I can roll over my 401(k) into other investments, right?"

"Look, Bill," I said, and paused for the right words. "I've got to tell you, based on what you've laid out for me so far, I don't think this is the right thing for you to do."

His face fell. "Sorry?"

"Have you burned any bridges since you announced you were going to retire?"

He looked at me hard, raised his eyebrows, and didn't give me any kind of definite "no." I could see the wheels turning. At last he said, "Maybe *one bridge* is starting to burn, but it hasn't completely torched."

I know he was picturing the retirement party his office had held for him at a nice restaurant, just a few days before our meeting. All his colleagues had come—those who had retired, and those still working. He was recalling the handshakes. The hugs. The toasts.

"Listen," I said. "I know this is hard. But even without doing the math, I don't think you are in a position to retire comfortably. Not without a major reduction in lifestyle, anyway. Not without creating some serious risk down the road. And from what I understand about your kind of work, I doubt you could come close to replacing your pay with a job at another company. Especially if you had to go back to work a few years from now."

He took another long pause before he said, "Well, that one bridge really *is* on fire. But I think I can put it out."

"Look," I said. "Sometimes it's unhealthy for people to keep working, depending on the environment. Nothing's worth your health. Why did you decide to retire at this time?"

I let him talk for a good long while at this point. Basically, his friends had retired and he was envious. Plus, a bunch of new people had come into the office, and his relationships with them were not as strong. Bottom line? The lure of "every day being a Saturday" had become too great. He simply *wanted to be retired,* like his friends.

I give Bill a huge amount of credit for even listening to me at that first meeting. He could have walked out and found another financial advisor that same afternoon, rolled over his money, retired, and not have had to face the anxiety I had created. Well, not faced it for a few years, anyway.

I could see how tough it would be for Bill to go back into the office and try to "unretire" now. How painful it would be to try to put the horse back in the barn. How truly humbling to announce your retirement, have your party, and then come back with your tail between your legs a few days later.

"Look," I said. "What if you go to the office and at least find out if you can put out the fire on that one bridge? Just see if it's possible. Find out if you *can* still get your job back."

Then I said something I often say: "Make me the bad guy. If someone asks, 'what the heck is going on,' blame it on *me.* Say, 'I sat down with my wealth manager, and he told me it was a bad idea to retire at this time. That I should become more financially sound before I actually stop working.'"

Lots of times, clients are faced with a very tough decision like this and are very uncomfortable making them. Allowing them to use me as the bad guy can really help facilitate an otherwise rough situation. Plus, most of the time I *am* the bad guy. I made the snowball, they're just throwing it.

Bill went away for a couple of days, and when he came back, he sat down again in my office with a look of strength and resolution, not defeat.

"I did it," he said. "I put out the fire. They said they'd take me back. It was probably the hardest thing I've ever had to do in my entire life, but I did it. What now?"

What now? I gave him a detailed game plan based on better future numbers and the three great risks. We looked at how his numbers actually had to pencil out to create a sustained *and growing* thirty-plus year income stream that he could live on. For starters, I said, "I don't want you to retire until your mortgage has been paid off and your daughter's educational costs are behind you."

It took Bill about five years to accomplish those tasks. Then, guess what? After a much more upbeat consultation, he did retire. We created a solid plan for thirty-plus years of full retirement, divided into the five-year investment segments you will learn about in this book. And yes, I did finally roll over and invest his 401(k) money, which had grown nicely.

I'm sure Bill held *another* retirement party five years later. It might have been somewhat lower key than the first shindig, but I know it proved a lot more satisfying in the long run.

INVESTING IS ACTUALLY THE EASY PART

"Risk comes from not knowing what you're doing."

—WARREN BUFFETT

Remember how the question, "How much of a nest egg do I need," wasn't the right question to start off your retirement planning? Well, maybe you're also beginning to see how the question, "Where should I invest my money," is not quite the right question either.

In fact, I often tell my clients, "Investing is the easy part." Believe me, once I helped Bill figure out the right pathway into his retirement, I did not find it difficult to figure out where to invest his 401(k) money. Most importantly, however, those decisions were *just another piece* of his overall planning.

The right question is bigger. You truly must ask yourself,

"What is my complete retirement game plan?" Because without a viable, well-considered, long-term strategy, you are going to make some foolish decisions. You are going to keep wavering from your path. And worse, you are going to be subject to mounting fears and uncertainties every single year of your retirement.

Your plan must account for the three great risks of timing, inflation, and longevity. It must ensure not just a sufficient nest egg, but also an adequate income from that nest egg every year for the rest of your life—whether or not you have a pension to back you up. Most importantly, your plan must deliver the most precious gift of retirement: confidence.

In this book, you will find such a plan. Carefully modeled. Based on sound statistics. And addressing all three of the great risks.

BUT WHY SHOULD YOU LISTEN TO ME?

At this point, you may be asking yourself, "Of all the people out there trying to give me advice, why should I listen to Sam Marrella?"

Well, I could tell you about my three decades of experience and the hundreds of people I've helped through their retirement journeys. My successes. My reputation. My outcomes. And I certainly *will* explain to you the simple math of my game plan. But I know that successfully and joyfully navigating the coming years of your life will take more than just strategizing with an expert.

It will take the right attitude.

I often talk to my clients, not just about escaping the fears that come with retiring, but about approaching this phase of their lives in the proper frame of mind altogether. I use stories from my own life, and they tell me these conversations help.

So, before we plunge into the art of wealth management and the specifics of the game plan, I want to tell you a couple of personal tales. Not just because I want you to get to know me better, but also so you understand my personal philosophy about "game planning," and what I think about the proper relationship between wealth manager and client.

These stories center on basketball.

CHAPTER 1

LESSONS FROM THE TOP OF THE KEY

"Confidence is something you create within yourself by believing in who you are."

—ANONYMOUS

Maybe you don't love basketball the way I love basketball. But it's hard to find a better sport to train you for life. Or personal finance.

I never played in the NBA or even any level above college. To begin with, I never grew past 5'9", and I could never slam dunk. Still, I was a heckuva high school player and a solid college player, and, for a time, basketball was the most important thing in my life.

I started young. Like me, my father was a wealth manager. But at the time, I was much more impressed that he moonlighted as a high school basketball referee. I'm pretty sure that refereeing was the tougher job.

When I was ten years old, I used to tag along to my dad's games. I looked forward not just to the action on the court, but also to following him into the locker room, where we'd mingle with the coaches and star players.

In the locker room, people were very nice to my dad. During the games, it was a different story.

Sitting in the bleachers, I had to listen to this father of mine, who I so much admired, get lit up. Literally, *just screamed at.* People rarely knew I was the referee's kid, so sometimes the people sitting right next to me would be yelling at him with the harshest language of all.

My dad unfortunately went bald at age twenty-three, so a favorite comment was, "Hey ref, did your hair get in your eyes? Because you really blew that one." At first, my feelings would get hurt. Sitting there, I'd clench my fists and want to punch somebody. But over time, I saw the *inevitability* of all the yelling and screaming. It was *unavoidable,* since 50% of the crowd was bound to dislike each and every call. And yes, sometimes he made calls where he deserved to be yelled at by the fans and the coaches. Hey, we all make mistakes, even my dad.

But I saw how he had to make sure that neither of those two *inevitabilities* stopped him from doing his job.

In the end, seeing my dad out there getting screamed at game after game turned out to be a good thing. I developed a thick skin at a young age—especially when I saw that no matter what happened, my dad never lost his cool. He was always calm, he was always composed, and he was always great with the kids. He'd tell them politely what they did wrong or sometimes complimented them on what they did right. Even better, sometimes he would admit, man to man, "I blew that one." And then he'd smile.

He'd say to me, "You know, you can learn everything you need to know about a person by watching them on the field of play."

In fact, on the way home from a game, my dad would often talk about the way a coach or a player had acted in a really good, sportsmanlike fashion. "I'd hire that guy," he'd say with certainty. "Did you see how well he handled himself despite a few calls that went against him? I fouled him out on a tough call—but he got up, handed me the ball, and didn't say a word."

Then we'd talk about the other guys. The guys who'd lost their cool, acted up, and had to be thrown out of the game.

But my dad was also a wealth manager. Like the doctors in those days, wealth managers made house calls, most often in the evenings. He was a busy guy, so I'd ask to go along for those rides, just to spend some time with him. He'd run around town, usually leaving me in the car—"I need to pop into this client's house for five minutes to get a couple of signatures."

An hour later—which to a ten year old seemed like ten hours—he'd emerge. Back in those days, there were no Gameboys, smartphones, or iPads to help pass the time.

Ever the gentleman, my dad would apologize: "I know that took longer than I expected, but they really needed my help with a few other issues. That's what I do. I help people. They're my clients and they pay me to help them, and I love it." He really wanted me to absorb that lesson. And I surely did.

Even at ten, I appreciated how important he was to his clients. Sometimes I'd sit quietly in the back during one of his living room meetings and I was amazed at how much a couple would appreciate his help.

"Man, dad," I'd say afterwards. "If you spend any more time with those clients they're going to ask you to be in their family portrait."

What I learned at those games and on those rides with my dad was far more important than anything I learned in any class in any school: A good player plays not for himself, but for his team. He respects everyone else in the game. He never loses his cool. Never loses his perspective. He leaves his losses in the past.

But I had a lot more to learn, both from basketball and from my dad.

THE ROLE OF THE POINT GUARD

"Basketball is a team game. But that doesn't mean all five players should have the same amount of shots."

—DEAN SMITH

When I was a kid, I never wanted to do anything except play hoops. But because I was small, I had to be faster and smarter than the bigger guys. I also had to learn to put up with the fact that the big guys got most of the attention both on and off the court. By the time I was a sophomore in high school, I was only 5'3", but thanks to coaches who saw some potential, I was inserted in the lineup as a point guard on the varsity team.

I only weighed 105 pounds at the time, and I looked more like I was twelve than fifteen; but, like my dad, I knew the game. And knowing the game counted for a lot.

What is a point guard? He or she has a very special role.

Of the five players you see running around on the court, the smallest guy is often the point guard. He (or she, on a women's team) acts like the quarterback of the team. He calls the plays and starts the offense. When a team is on the court, the coach can't be out there telling everyone what to do, because he's stuck on the sidelines. The point guard is the guy who is in the middle of the action, trying to do the thinking for everyone and acting as an extension of the coach on the court. He has the moment-to-moment tactical responsibility—making sure that the other players are in the right positions, getting the ball to the scorers, and executing the game plan.

Good communications matter as much in basketball as in the rest of life, and you can think about the point guard as the lead communicator on the team. He calls the plays, lets everyone know where to be, and tries to put his teammates in position to succeed.

Now, the point guard is rarely himself a high scorer. He's out there to *set up* the high scorers. In basketball, if you make a good pass to a teammate that leads him to a score, it's called an "assist" or a "helper." You're helping *someone else* score for the whole team.

Not a lot of people want to play point guard because they usually want to be the big scorers themselves. They want their pictures in the paper. They want the cheerleaders to know their name. They want to be the star. But if you ask a coach who is the most important player on the court, they will usually say, "It's the point guard."

As for me, I loved playing the point. I truly loved making a good pass to help a teammate score. Nothing gave me more satisfaction than a guy pointing at me and saying, "Thanks for setting me up, man. Good pass." I enjoyed that more than scoring myself. I took pride in being a great teammate. That was far more important to me than being known to the crowd as a great player.

THE CURE FOR *NEWSPAPER EYES*

"In the future, everyone will be world-famous for 15 minutes."

—ANDY WARHOL

In spite of my humble role as point guard, I *was* once the star of a basketball game, with my name in the paper and all that came with it. But that experience turned into one of the most traumatic and important lessons of my life. Sure it was "just high school ball," but even four decades later, I carry the lesson of one excruciating weekend with me every day, in both my work and private life.

I already mentioned that my role as a point guard was on the varsity team. Well, I made it to varsity as a sophomore. If you know anything about high school ball, you know that was a big deal. Very few kids move up from junior varsity to varsity their sophomore year.

Here's the story I call *Newspaper Eyes.*

We were playing a rival team at home on a Friday night. It was a big game, crucial to getting us into the playoffs. Coming down the stretch, we were down two points with about a minute to go. I went backdoor and made a layup, to tie the game. The opponents came down and missed their shot. We got the ball. Or rather, *I got the ball* at the top of the key with about fifteen seconds left on the clock. We had another guard who was a three-year starter—but I saw he'd run and hid in the corner. That meant I didn't have a choice, I had to try to make a play.

By the grace of God, I drove to the basket and made a really good pass to a teammate who laid it in, got fouled, and then made the foul shot too.

We won by three points and the place went crazy. The seniors on the team even invited me to join them at the local Pizza Hut after the game. No big deal? Wrong. Getting invited to Pizza Hut by the seniors was a real big deal for a sophomore. It was rare that a sophomore got invited to hang with the seniors. More often, they'd beat us up, just for fun.

The thing I remember most about that trip to Pizza Hut wasn't the pizza, it was the fact that the senior cheerleaders actually knew my name. I felt really good afterwards and went home for my post-game ritual. That ritual was my dad and I breaking down the game and me getting his assessment of how I played.

That pow-wow went well and, as you now understand, that meant the world to me. He was my biggest fan, but he was also a true student of the game and he never hesitated to tell me when I messed up or didn't play well. So, at age fifteen, to have my dad praise me after his post-game review—well, that really was the icing on the cake of a great night. (Decades later, I did exactly the same with my son, who was a high school and college point guard, as well.)

When I got up that Saturday morning long ago, I glanced at the local newspaper, and there was my name! In fact, the story mentioned me several times! Game-winning pass, etc., etc.

Later that morning, I went to Saturday practice as a new man. I was glowing. Confident and maybe, just maybe, a little bit cocky. It seemed like a whole new chapter of my life was opening up.

Then, about an hour into practice, I turned the ball over. I made a bad pass. That happens when you are the point guard and you have the ball a lot of the time. Just one bad pass—I threw the ball out of bounds. I thought my teammate was going in one direction and he was going in another. Totally my fault. It's always the passer's fault.

And then what happens? The head coach absolutely loses his mind. The coach was an ex-Marine. Tough as nails. (A great coach, too. Ended his career with over 500 wins and is in the Pennsylvania Sports Hall of Fame.) He blows his whistle at the top of his lungs at least five times and a total quiet falls over the gym. Everybody in the gym has stopped in their tracks as he yells out, "Hey, Newspaper Eyes. Yeah, you. Newspaper Eyes."

He glares at me as he stomps toward me. "You make a couple good plays, and now you're reading your press clippings. Then you come to my practice and all of a sudden you think you're a big deal. You've got a big head, and I've got to give you the bad news, *you are not that good.* As a matter of fact, you're not even good enough to be on varsity. I don't even know why I gave you a varsity uniform."

Now, keep in mind that I was being verbally undressed in front of twenty-four of my teammates, varsity and junior varsity alike. Remember the seniors, the ones who invited me to go with them to Pizza Hut twelve hours earlier? They were biting through their lips trying not to burst out into laughter.

The name of the JV coach was Skip, and he and the JVs were at the other end of the court. The coach screams, "Skip, get this kid out of my sight. He's not varsity material. He's not good enough to play varsity. He's nothing but a JV player." I then proceeded to embark on the walk of shame. The long arduous walk to the JV end of the court. It was only seventy feet, but it felt like seventy miles, especially *in front of your boys.*

I was speechless.

My silence continued when I returned home and my dad asked, "How did practice go?"

"I don't want to talk about it," I said.

His expression fell. "What do you mean?" He saw me play the night before and excel down the stretch. He'd read the same newspaper that very morning, and he was expecting to hear about the coach's happy reaction to the Friday night game.

I said, "Dad, I'm on JV now. It's a long story. I really don't want to talk about it."

I remember him just looking at me, not asking for more details.

The remaining hours of that weekend were among the longest of my life. I hid in my room, too embarrassed to go out. Over and over, I replayed the scene of being taken down in front of all my peers—*the same guys who had asked me to the Pizza Hut!*

Lying on my bed staring at the ceiling, I said to myself, "I *did* read the newspaper. I *was* feeling good about myself. The coach was just *waiting* for me to mess up. He's some kind of crazy *amateur psychologist.* At some point during practice, he knew that I was *certain* to throw the ball away. It was *inevitable.* And whether I messed up five minutes or two hours into practice, he was ready to pounce. To show me and everyone...*what?*"

Come practice Monday afternoon, I dutifully put on my old JV gear and headed into the gym to practice with the JV team. But the varsity coach, the big ex-Marine, calls me over. And what does he do? He starts yelling at me, again. Only now he shouts:

"What, you don't think you're good enough to be on varsity?"

I knew better than to respond.

"Go get your varsity stuff on. I hope you learned a lesson over the weekend."

Forty years later, I'm still mulling that lesson—but my dad understood it right away. Most parents would have marched down to the school and tried to get the guy fired for mistreating their kid. But my dad just laughed and said, "You know what? He's trying to make a man out of you. As far as I'm concerned, this is just another hurdle placed in your path. You go back to practice. You bust your butt and you get back in his good graces."

And you know what? I did. That ex-Marine coach and I finished out the year together—and *then* he got fired. Another kid's father allegedly complained to the school board about the way the coach yelled at his son. It was a real shame, because that prevented him from teaching life lessons to so many others.

BASKETBALL AS A WAY OF LIFE

"Basketball is not just a game, it's a way of life."

—SAM MARRELLA

In sports, when you earn a big win, if you get too euphoric you tend not to do well in future games. When you suffer a big loss, if you look for excuses and lose your confidence, you won't win future games either. You have to remember that it's all about the *long-term* outcome.

The same is true in personal finance. You have to overcome the emotional high of the big wins, and you have to overcome the adversity of the tough losses—because, either way, you will have to get up and play your next game the very best way you can.

Maybe my high school coach was rightly fired for treating his players the way he did. But as for me, I'm grateful to him to this day. He surely prevented me from ever again falling prey to "Newspaper Eyes." No matter my successes or failures, remembering that one weekend will always keep me in balance. From that event and from so many other basketball experiences, I learned how the world can build you up and give you a false sense of security—and then, just as quickly, take you down for mistakes you are *sure* to make.

I was not fated to play basketball in later life, but I like to think that basketball represents my *way* of life: grit, teamwork, and helping others succeed.

WHEN E.F. HUTTON SPEAKS...

I applied that attitude right out of college, when I started at the brokerage firm E.F. Hutton. I could have gone to work with my dad, but he insisted that I broaden my experience by working for a big firm.

And therein lies another tale.

E.F. Hutton had a famous tagline that still resonates: "When E.F. Hutton speaks, people listen." They'd run TV commercials in which two guys would be chatting at a table in a restaurant. One would say, "My broker's E.F. Hutton, and E.F. Hutton says..." And the whole restaurant would lean over to listen in on the conversation.

But right before I signed on, E.F. Hutton was involved in a highly publicized scandal. So, by my first day in training in New York, the famous tagline had become a national joke.

A dark cloud had formed over the three-week training session—and brought gloom even to my hotel room. There I had two roommates, one sixty-five and one fifty-nine. Both had been around the block many times in many different businesses, and had this world-weary feel about them. Both were trying to make a late career change.

Me, I was twenty-two, but looked eighteen. I remember the fifty-nine year old, a guy who'd been a kind of nomadic salesman his whole life, laughing when he saw me. He smirked and said, "So, kid, what do you want to be when you grow up?"

"A financial advisor," I replied without a trace of humor or irony. "That's why I'm here. I want to help people make good decisions with their money."

It was high school all over: the skeptical coaches. Having to keep my eye on the ball. Having to compete with older, more experienced players.

Fine, I thought. *I love the competition. If no one's keeping score, I'm not interested.* That son of a gun wasn't discouraging, he was motivating. And in fact, I knew that he was the one starting this career from scratch, not me. I'd grown up seeing my father make those late night house calls. And I had already played point guard.

The E.F. Hutton job required a huge amount of cold calling to drum up business. Because I really did look eighteen, it wasn't easy to gain people's trust—and I was best on the phone. I'd call people from a long list and go into my pitch, trying to get them to talk to me. If you've ever made cold calls, you know it's a tough play. You *will* get yelled at and you *will* get ridiculed and hung up on. And you *will* get sixty nos for every yes. A low-scoring game, but those were the rules.

Most people can't handle the word no. But by now, you can see that I was used to getting flack. I was used to hearing no. Compared to being razzed in the locker room for being a midget? Compared to getting verbally sucker-punched by an ex-Marine? Compared to seeing my dad get yelled at by a gym full of angry spectators? No big deal. *I got this,* I said to myself.

And when I got that single positive response of the day and landed a new client? Great, now let's get back to work. One down, hundreds to go.

I saw I was far better off because of the hurdles I had to overcome than the people who'd been handed everything on a silver platter. I hung in there, and I did succeed, even as E.F. Hutton collapsed and got sold.

Just one more thing I learned from being the "little guy" in basketball:

I learned that whenever you get an opportunity to succeed, you'd better seize it. Big guys in basketball and rich guys in the financial world might get a dozen chances, but if you're the little guy or the guy with modest means, you'd better take advantage of the far fewer opportunities that will come your way.

Is that unfair? Of course. When you're a big guy and you mess up, you're just having a bad day. When you're a little guy and you mess up, you're fulfilling somebody's prophecy that you were too small and weak all along. But it's nobody's job except yours to change that prophecy.

That's not complaining. That's understanding the game.

THE LIFE ASSIST

"Life is really simple, but we insist on making it complicated."

—CONFUCIUS

Nowadays, I'm still playing point guard.

In fact, as of this writing, my dad is seventy-nine and he's still a wealth manager. So is my brother. We fulfilled a family dream when we went into business together about fifteen years ago. My dad has been doing this for fifty years, my brother for twenty-five, and me for over thirty.

You remember how the purpose of the point guard in basketball was to set up the other players to score? To make an "assist?" Well, as a wealth manager, that's pretty much my job. It means I'm still the on-court coach—not just giving advice, but facilitating communication and making day-to-day tactical calls for my clients.

As I pointed out in the Introduction, the calls required from a wealth manager involve much more than investment decisions. So, in the next chapter we'll go into some detail about *holistic wealth management*.

But for now, let's just say it's my job to provide a "life assist."

As this book progresses, you will see that I have structured *Your Retirement Game Plan* to take into account the inevitable ups and downs of the financial world you are certain to see over the next thirty years.

If you want to play basketball, you can't control your height, but you can control how well you handle the ball. If you want to retire comfortably, you may not be able to control the size of your initial savings, but you can invest those savings wisely to create long-term income.

I built the game plan to control what you *can* control, given a full understanding of what you *cannot* control.

The big score will be confidence.

CHAPTER 2

HOLISTIC WEALTH MANAGEMENT

"Shouldn't you fix that hole in your roof?"

"Well, right now it's raining. And when it ain't raining, it don't bother me none."

—ANONYMOUS

Do you plan for the future? Or is the future too far away?

Most people do eventually get around to planning for their retirement. But few seem to realize that the longer they wait, the fewer options and less control they will have over the quality of that retirement. Later we will explore, mathematically, the risks associated with retirement timing. But trust me, all the math works better if you fix the hole in your roof *before* the rain arrives.

Unfortunately, when people do finally create their plans, they rarely start with any fundamental understanding of what it takes to build a thirty-plus year retirement. They may have a 401(k) plan through their work, some passive accounts, and a scattering of market investments—but most have no comprehensive strategy.

These same people usually have plenty of other skills. They may be terrific doctors or lawyers, tennis players or plumbers, airline pilots or warehouse managers. But personal financial planning was never a part of their college curriculum, their professional boards, or their on-the-job training.

That's why they come to people like me.

The game plan can work without professional assistance, but in this chapter and the next, I want to explain the process and value of working closely with a wealth manager. A person like myself can help you define your goals and create a strategy not just for your best possible active years, but your best possible retirement years—given your individual means and circumstances. He or she can help you implement that strategy and stay with it over time.

Even if you decide not to work with a pro, you could benefit from reading through this section to make sure you understand the scope of the planning you should do on your own.

I practice what is called *holistic wealth management* in a highly structured way. I break out my work into three distinct areas. Let me explain with a little chalkboard "algebra" from the financial planning world.

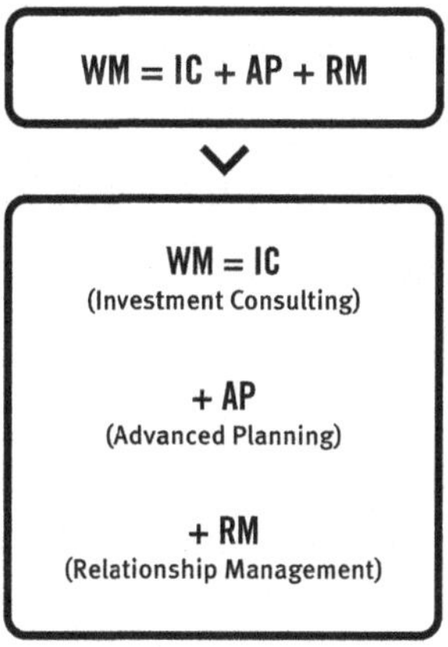

The WM on the chalkboard, of course, stands for wealth management. But I should probably start by saying that wealth management isn't just for the kind of people we usually consider "wealthy."

Most of my clients are ordinary folks who have worked hard, lived within their means, and saved money. They have followed a very simple formula: They spent less than they had earned and invested the difference. Year after year after year. Rinse, wash, repeat.

Over the course of a thirty- or forty-year career, they have managed to create a million dollars or more of net worth in 2017 dollars. They are truly "the millionaires next door."

Surprisingly, it's not always the people you think *should* be wealthy who actually manage to pull this off. Plenty of doctors, professional athletes, successful musicians, and other high-income professionals live beyond their means, and don't actually have a million or more put away when they near retirement. High spending seems to go with the territory.

So, when I talk about wealth management, I don't mean planning for rich people. I mean holistic planning for *anyone's* assets, income, and risks. And I include planning for things like charitable giving, for disability, and for transferring wealth to the next generation.

INVESTMENT COUNSELING

"Retired: Gainfully unemployed and proud of it."

—ANONYMOUS

We'll start breaking down our three big categories with IC, investment consulting, because that's probably why you picked up this book in the first place. IC represents the traditional work of the financial planner with the additional element of *long-term planning*. But if I do my job, I'll get you to pay attention to the advance planning (AP) and relationship management (RM) stuff, too.

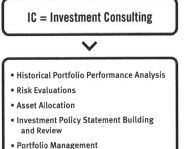

IC = Investment Consulting

- Historical Portfolio Performance Analysis
- Risk Evaluations
- Asset Allocation
- Investment Policy Statement Building and Review
- Portfolio Management
  It is a verbal description of how all this moves toward goal fulfillment aligned with stated values.

When I start working with a client, I'll look at the historical performance of their current portfolio and see if it makes sense with a sensible retirement game plan based on secure income streams.

Then I'll evaluate their situation for the three great risks of timing, inflation, and longevity.

Next, I'll work on allocating or re-allocating their assets.

This includes creating an investment policy statement to underlie their overall game plan—usually the segmented investment strategy you will see in Chapter 6.[2]

Then my firm will take over active management of a client's portfolio.

I will go into much detail on allocating retirement funds to different types of investment strategies but, as I said earlier, investment counseling is usually the easy part of my job.

A LOT TO CONSIDER UNDER *AP*

"Wealth is not about having a lot of money it's about having a lot of options."

—CHRIS ROCK

Now we get to the real difference between wealth management and financial planning.

2 Diversification and asset allocation do not ensure a profit or protect against a loss.

AP = WE + WT + WP + CG

WE = **Wealth Enhancement** (tax and cash flow planning)

The investment plan is completed during IC, which includes Asset Allocation (both current and recommended).

WT = **Wealth Transfer** (transferring wealth effectively; may not be within a family)

WP = **Wealth Protection** (risk mitigation, legal structures, and transferring risk to insurance company)

CG = **Charitable Giving**

The first important piece of advanced planning (AP) is wealth enhancement (WE). Remember that we identified inflation as one of the great risks for retirees. Unless your wealth continues to grow *both before and during* retirement, you are going to have plenty of rain coming in through your roof.

But wealth enhancement requires not just the investment and income piece, but careful tax and cash flow planning, as well. We need to ensure that we mitigate the amount of taxes you pay to the government. It is not what you earn but what you keep that is most important to your long-term financial success—and to achieving all that is important to you and your family.

That means some number crunching, tax law research,[3] and budgeting.

Now, most people hate taxes, but they *really* hate budgeting. And once they've done a budget, they *really, really* hate keeping to that budget. If you will forgive me another quotation at this point, I have to add one of my favorites, source unknown:

"A budget tells us what we can't afford, but it doesn't keep us from buying it."

People know cheeseburgers and French fries are not good for them. They know eating such things will make them gain weight. But they do it anyway. Why? "Because cheeseburgers and fries taste so good!"

Then, a week later, they say, "Dang, I gained weight. I wonder how that happened?"

It's no different with a personal budget. People know they should not take that overseas trip or lease that sports car, but they do it anyway. Why? Because they think the future is the future, and the present is now. *And right now, it ain't raining.*

---

3 You should discuss any tax or legal matters with the appropriate professional.

A good wealth manager knows that *the future is now*. He or she knows that the decisions you make this minute will create your future, and it's the wealth manager's job to help you separate emotion from fact. Lots of people, whether or not they can hold to a diet, come to wealth managers to help them plan their lifestyle budget. They know they need not just our expertise, but also our reality check on their fiscal emotions.

Let me remind you that I have placed personal budgeting not under risk mitigation, but under wealth enhancement. Whether you hire a wealth manager, I suggest you use the same terminology. If you think about *not* taking that trip to Australia as a *positive* step toward the WE in our equation, maybe you'll head for the Grand Canyon instead.

PROTECTING YOURSELF AND YOUR HEIRS: WT + WP

The second big piece of advanced planning is wealth transfer or WT on the blackboard. About 55% of Americans die intestate—without a will. But writing a will is only the beginning of a sound wealth transfer plan. As a wealth manager, I make sure that you construct an effective estate plan. I know that without such a plan, updated regularly, it's unlikely that all of your assets will move forward to the next generation in the way you would like them to.

In my work, I see many tragic situations caused by a failure to do proper estate planning. Let's look at just one example.

A very nice couple I advised were married for twenty years, then got into a terrible fight and rushed into a divorce. Only one month later, they reconciled. That *could* have led to a happy ending, but *they never officially remarried.*

Sadly, several years later the husband contracted cancer. I met with him and strongly advised him that because his wife was no longer legally his wife it would create a severe consequence for their estate taxes. She would be treated as a non-family member and would be subject to a 15% state inheritance tax on their entire retirement plan.

This fellow had spent his whole working life saving for retirement. Because neither he nor his wife had a pension, their income came solely from their two Social Security checks and the income generated from their retirement plan. I advised him to urgently see an attorney for sound legal advice surrounding remarriage, and to get his estate planning documents updated. He loved his spouse, but he never got around to it. He never changed his marital status and by law, she was not officially his spouse.

When he died, this poor woman had to withdraw significant portions of their retirement funds to pay the inheritance taxes. Oh, and by the way, to make matters worse, she had to *pay federal income taxes on the money she withdrew to pay the state inheritance taxes.* The math went something like this: She had to withdraw $75,000 from their IRA to pay the state. Then, because that $75,000 was counted as taxable income, she had to take *another* almost $20,000 out to pay Uncle Sam! As a result, much of the hard work and prudent investing her husband had put into planning their retirement was wiped out—all because he did not take some basic legal steps.

Bottom line: You have to address *all* the factors of wealth management in your game plan. None can be ignored.

Most people simply don't have the time to acquire this expertise and do their own estate planning. They're too busy creating an estate in the first place. Or, as in the case of the husband who contracted cancer, dealing with an illness or other major life event.

PROTECTING YOUR WEALTH FROM BEING UNJUSTLY TAKEN AWAY

Wealth protection, the WP part of the equation, means mitigating or transferring the risks that threaten your assets whenever possible. People can work hard their whole lives, then see their nest eggs wiped out by a lawsuit, a disability, or a bad tax liability. Often, such tragedies can be prevented with the right forethought and some manageable insurance premiums.

For example, anyone who has a million or more dollars in assets should consider an umbrella insurance policy. If you are in a car accident, your auto insurance offers you some protection, but it's usually not enough. Lawyers search for money, and if they find it in your bank account, they will do everything in their power to get into that bank account. Umbrella insurance, a kind of expanded liability insurance, is not expensive. As a wealth manager, I will definitely fit it into your budget.

Another important risk faced by everyone is the possibility of a disability or illness requiring long-term care. It's not unusual for a nursing home to charge as much as $12,000 a month, and it's unlikely that your existing health insurance policy provides any long-term care coverage.

In my line of work, I've seen plenty of kids who expected to see an inheritance come away with nothing. Why? Because all the money was consumed in the last few years of their parents' lives due to their needed long-term care.

In my experience, long-term care and disability insurances often proves more important than life insurance. When you die, people will cry a little bit and come to your funeral, but you will no longer be an expense to your family. If you become disabled or need long-term care, you will become a burden to your family, both financially and otherwise. Every situation is different and requires personalized attention to these issues, but everyone needs to address this concern.

Other kinds of wealth protection may include insurance related to your business, along with trust designations related to business decisions, in case you're incapacitated. As a wealth manager, I will work with qualified estate planning attorneys, look at all your individual circumstances, and see where firewalls need to be built.

Wealth preservation can be complicated, somewhat confusing, and not any fun to deal with, but that WP is an essential element to your wealth management plan. As your wealth manager, I find it imperative that your wealth not be unjustly taken from you and your family.

CHARITY WORKS BETTER WHEN PLANNED

You may have charitable intentions, which you have included in your will. It's wonderful to provide money to charities when you die, but by utilizing certain planning strategies, you can also receive some lucrative tax benefits from giving to charities while you are still alive.

Best of all, you get to watch the charities enjoy and do great things with your gifts.

A good wealth manager will help you make a much bigger difference in the world by using the available financial tools to maximize your "CG," lower your tax bill, and leverage your long-term assets. Like most things in life, charity works a lot better when you make it part of an overall strategy.

RM: A LONG-TERM AFFAIR

"Great things in business are never done by one person. They're done by a team of people."

—STEVE JOBS

The third, and maybe most important factor in the wealth management equation I wrote on the blackboard is RM, or relationship management. There are two parts to this strategy: the relationship between a wealth manager and a client, and the relationship between a wealth manager and the bigger world of professional expertise. Both are fundamental.

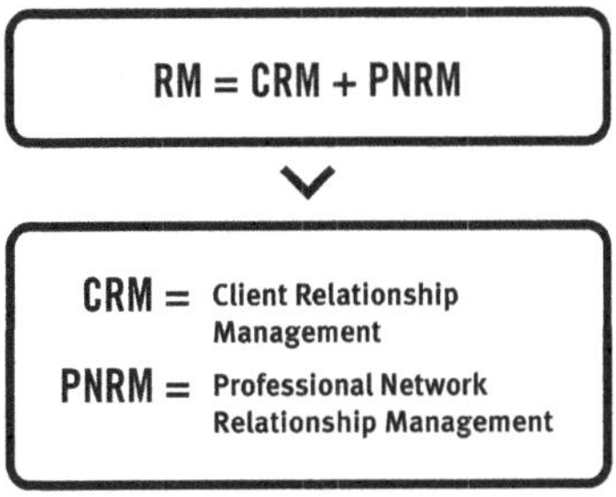

As a wealth manager, I am not interested in short-term affairs. I'm not interested in setting up your game plan and then stepping away. For starters, I know that any serious game plan needs professional monitoring and that adjustments need to be made over time. But I also see it as my role as your point guard to be your coach on the court until the buzzer sounds.

Earlier in this book, I spoke about managing one's emotions, both the highs and the lows. I touched on the way a wealth manager can help in that effort. But since we're deep into algebra right now, let me now describe my relationship with three constants:

I am a *Confidant, Steward,* and *Advocate.*

In the Introduction, I told the story of Bill, and how I helped him make a decision to reverse his retirement. In that tale, I was acting as a *confidant.* Bill didn't know it when he walked into my office, but he really needed a confidant—an unemotional third party with whom he could talk through his situation.

I know you want to be heard—and I must say, too many people who do wealth managing don't understand that simple truth. Too many spend an inordinate amount of their time doing most of the talking. In Chapter 1, I wanted to give you some of my personal story so you'd get to know me. But if you meet with me in my office, I'm going to ask you a lot of questions and *listen*—because I am intently interested in getting to know you. Who is important to you? What are your goals? Wishes? Dreams? Only then can I help you achieve what's important to you and your family.

Here's another favorite quote every wealth manager should keep in mind. Opinions vary on who said this first, but it has always resonated with me:

"God gave us two ears and one mouth for a reason—we should use them in proportion."

STEWARDSHIP

I also play the role of *steward*. If you picked up this book, you probably know the burden of working as both chief executive officer and chief financial officer (CEO and CFO) for your family. Your spouse, your children, and even your grandchildren may be highly dependent on the decisions you make. Few people possess the necessary financial expertise—*on top of their own professional expertise*—to make such decisions properly. And certainly not across the whole range of financial issues they face.

As you head toward retirement, these issues become more complicated and occur more frequently. You discover that you must not merely address your portfolio, but all the attendant factors I described under advanced planning. As stewards of our clients' wealth, our firm helps them make smart financial decisions, then implement and track those decisions over time. Our aim is to relieve our clients of the burden of making such decisions alone.

ADVOCACY

Finally, I play the role of *advocate.* Wealth managers rarely emphasize this role, but it can be crucial for many clients. For example, a client may be the beneficiary of a trust and have to work with a trust officer. This client may ask us to make an argument to his trust officer in which we *advocate* for him. For example, we might say to the officer, "Our wealth management firm worked with the grantors of this trust, our client's parents, for thirty years. They would not have approved of him buying a Bentley, but they would have been fine with him driving a BMW."

We act as advocates—or champions—for our clients in a wide variety of legal and financial matters, both simple and complex. We can do this effectively because we know the laws, the financial lingo, and have a full understanding of our client's situation. We often know to ask questions that our client would never have considered, and we make our client's arguments from a position of acknowledged expertise.

PNRM MATTERS TOO

As a wealth manager, I also give serious attention to my relationship with my network of fellow professionals, my continuing education into the complex world of finance, and my tracking of the never-ending changes in tax law, financial technology, and investment strategy. I do this because it leads to better outcomes. Wealth managers are in the outcome business and you deserve the best outcomes possible.

In our day-to-day work, my firm maintains contact with an army of the finest accountants, lawyers, estate planners, and other professionals we can find. This allows us to help you complete the wealth management puzzle.

But we also attend a lot of conferences and seminars. We're sitting in classrooms and learning a lot of new material. We know that without this effort, our educations and strategies would become out-of-date quickly.

We do try to involve you in the learning as best we can. I like to say that you don't necessarily need to know how to build a clock, but you should make sure you know how to tell time. At the very least, our clients need assurance that *we* are keeping up with the art of clock making. And I know you will appreciate it when we list the conferences we've recently attended, the courses we've recently completed, and the panels on which we have served. So do our fellow professionals.

Like all good relationships, PNRM, professional network relational management, requires constant attention.

A WORD ABOUT TRUST

Way back at the beginning of this chapter, when I explained IC, or investment consulting, I mentioned that the last step in the IC process was the transfer of client assets into our care.

If you have never worked with a wealth manager, that step might have given you pause.

While I strongly advocate the use of outside help to

manage your game plan, you do have to perform some due diligence. Just remember that the media lives for stories like Bernie Madoff, the "financial guru" who stole billions from his clients. At the same time, the media ignores the good, honest, day-to-day work performed by tens of thousands of reputable firms. As a result, people often let their suspicions prevent them from taking vital steps for their own well-being.

Personally, I never expect anyone to trust me before they know me. They may come in through a direct referral, or they may have heard good things second hand, but we have to meet in person to see if we connect. My family has been doing wealth management in a fairly small town for over fifty years. People know us. You may not have the luxury of finding a company like that, but please, don't let the fear factor stop you from working with a pro. A lot of controls have been put in place that make it pretty hard for a wealth manager to do bad things with your money.

I also have to say that before I take on clients, I have to trust them as well. When we meet, I also have to feel that we can develop a long-term relationship and that I can make a difference for you and your family.

AVOIDING A TRAIN CRASH

I remember one initial meeting with a guy who came in with his girlfriend. He ignored my efforts to get a complete picture of his situation, and he only wanted to talk about the $500,000 he wanted to invest. Again and again he felt the need to say it out loud: "$500,000." At the time, this was a pretty tidy sum, but he acted like he had cornered the market on money. I wasn't clear why his girlfriend was there, unless his goal was to impress her with this number.

Then he started talking about "several other investment advisors he had interviewed."

"Two of them said they can get me 12% or 15% on my $500,000," he said. "What kind of returns can you get for me?"

"With all due respect," I said politely, "I need to say that a lot of people have $500,000 to invest, and very, very few earn those kinds of returns. If I were you, and somebody told me they could get 12% or 15%, I would invest my money with them. Because I can't do that. Nor would I want to create an expectation that unrealistic."

I had been in the business long enough to know that if I were to engage in a relationship with a man like that, it would end badly. When you watch a movie that ends in a train crash, and then you watch it again, you can be pretty sure it will end in yet another train crash.

That meeting lasted exactly eight minutes. Afterwards, my assistant asked, "Your first meetings usually last at least an hour. What happened?"

"All I can tell you," I replied, "is that I saved myself fifty-two minutes."

As a wealth manager, I have to earn my clients' trust, and they have to earn mine.

CHAPTER 3

FACING THE THREE GREAT RISKS

"Failure occurs for two reasons:

1. *Doing things without thinking about them.*
2. *Thinking about things without doing them."*

—ANONYMOUS

Any retirement plan must effectively deal with all three of the risks I talked about in the Introduction. Any single risk or any combination of bad outcomes could spell a greatly reduced standard of living as you age.

Let's look a little more closely at these risks so you can understand how I designed the game plan to counter them.

RISK #1: TIMING

"The essence of strategy is choosing what not to do."

—PROF. MICHAEL PORTER

For starters, you have to choose the right time in your personal savings and career arc to retire. I've already given you a couple of examples of folks who tried to retire too soon.

But what about the condition of the financial markets in the year you retire? If you allocate your investments poorly, a significant downturn just after you choose to retire could endanger your entire thirty-year plan because the starting point matters much more than other checkpoints along the years.

When we look at the outcome probabilities of retirement in Chapter 5, you will see how you must preserve your wealth early in your retirement if you want to create sufficient income streams throughout your retirement.

If you retire just prior to a downturn in the market, your timing risk goes way up, because: 1) Your portfolio, if entirely invested in stocks, will shrink and may not generate sufficient income. 2) You will be tempted to sell your stocks in order to maintain your current income. 3) You may even be tempted to liquidate your portfolio entirely.

4) When the market recovers, which it has done in the past, your assets will likely be depleted.

HYPOTHETICAL DISASTER

To see the problem more clearly, let's look at a quick hypothetical.

Say you have been building a nest egg and have most of it invested in stocks. When you retire, you have a vague, general plan to sell stock as needed to fund your lifestyle, but you haven't looked very far down the road.

Unfortunately, you happen to retire in a year when the market takes a large dip.

Suppose you need to generate $1,000 a month from your stock portfolio to supplement your other income. Your plan is to sell shares each month to meet your needs. If in the first month of your retirement, your stock is valued at $10 a share, you will have to sell 100 shares, or 100 x $10 to meet your goal of $1,000.

But suppose next month the stock price falls to just $8. To get your necessary $1,000 in month two, you will have to sell 125 shares. And what if in month three, the price falls to $5? You will then have to sell 200 shares to fund your $1,000. If stocks continue to drop, you could get into real trouble.

Now suppose that two years later, stock prices recover. *Unfortunately, this rebound may no longer help you.* Since you were forced to sell off the majority of your stock, you now only hold a small fraction of your original position. If you had been able to hold on, you would have been okay, but now your shares are gone forever and can no longer fund your income.

When you started, you thought your money was likely to last the rest of your life. But because you got the timing wrong, your money will not last. It's that simple.

Does "getting the timing right" mean you should be buying and selling to try to "time" the market? No. That is clearly *not* the message. As the famous saying goes, "The Market Timing Hall of Fame has no members!"

You cannot predict whether the year in which you retire will be good or bad for the market. Instead, *Your Retirement Game Plan* is designed to account for inadvertently choosing a down-market year in which to retire.

RISK #2: INFLATION

"Inflation is taxation without legislation."

—MILTON FRIEDMAN

The rising cost of living over time inevitably means that you will have to create additional income as your retirement progresses. Even more importantly, inflation means that you may find yourself digging into your principal when you should not.

Inflation may not seem that significant from year to year, but it *inevitably becomes* significant over time. To see how, you need only compare the cost of a car fifteen years ago to the cost now. Movies, restaurants, and hotels will all tell the same story. Or, in most states, your property taxes. If I want to see how inflation has impacted me, I need only compare the real estate tax bill I received when I purchased my home seventeen years ago to the one I receive now.

Healthcare inflation probably represents the greatest single escalating cost in most American's budgets. Healthcare typically inflates at *twice* the rate of other vital, basic expenses. Regardless of political changes in Washington, this escalation will likely continue to impact you.

If you rely on a fixed or relatively fixed source of income

such as a pension or Social Security, inflation represents a major threat indeed. In essence, your current lifestyle will cost you more each and every year. As your regular expenses increase because of inflation, you end up with less and less money to spend on fun things. Things like eating out, traveling, and spoiling your grandkids.

Although Social Security income does adjust over time, these adjustments rarely match the actual rate of inflation. In the three years before this writing, Social Security has increased very little: 0% for two years, and just 0.2% in year three. That's because the macro-economic calculations used by the government have indicated no inflation at all.

Despite such "calculations," anyone who has gone to the grocery store knows that food costs have risen dramatically over the same time frame. Rising food costs especially impact retirees, because a favorite pastime for retirees is going out to eat. If prices are higher at the grocery store, what do you think happened at restaurants? The cost of dining out has also risen dramatically, but the government has chosen not to notice this dynamic.

Your retirement game plan must provide for increasing, not decreasing revenues over time.

RISK #3: LONGEVITY

"Life well spent is long."

—LEONARDO DA VINCI

Let me just say that I am in favor of a long life. I find it a highly desirable goal. But as a financial guy, I have to admit that longevity represents a big risk.

Many people alive today are projected to live to 120 or more.[4] No kidding. People a lot smarter than me are making these projections.

Medical science and technology continue to advance at a bewildering rate. Stem-cell therapy alone will create major possibilities for a longer life. And folks in white coats are experimenting with things like the 3D printing of new body organs. That means we all may have access to spare parts in the future. Yikes, that's going to make my job a lot harder!

Your game plan must account for you living a longer life than you ever expected to live.

4 Source: Peter Diamandis, Human Longevity, Inc.

EMOTIONAL CONTROL

"Calmness is power."

—JAMES ALLEN

I said earlier that I consider "fear" the fourth great risk for retirees. Certainly, it's my greatest challenge in working with clients.

In early 2009, following the market crash in 2008, I had a client come in to tell me that he wanted to sell everything. He'd been watching the market drop day after day, and finally he cracked. He said, "I understand why we're invested the way we are, but I just can't take the pain anymore."

Not only was the market trading horribly, but the media rhetoric made it sound like the world—or at least the financial world—was coming to an end. The phrase "Second Great Depression" was being thrown around without caution, and plenty of talking heads were saying that the second big one might be worse than the first.

My client had received three or four statements showing his portfolio had lost value, and he was panicked.

I sat him down in my office, looked him straight in the eye, and said, "Let's just reflect back on how this whole process started. Why did you come to me in the first place?"

His answer was succinct: "I wanted to grow my money so I could retire someday. I realized that the income streams from my small pension and Social Security would not be enough."

"Okay," I said. "We created a retirement game plan. Then we invested your assets for the long term as the plan suggested—*not for you to use this minute.* We talked from the outset about how there would be economic disruptions from time to time. We knew that you, like everyone, would experience occasional down drafts in your portfolio. But because you are invested for the long term and *for your retirement,* we knew that we would have to fight through these tough times. If you liquidate your portfolio now, will you have enough money to retire comfortably?"

"No," he admitted.

"Doesn't it make sense for us to stay the course? Keep to the plan we created years ago, and fight through this tough economic time?"

At last, I did get him to calm down. He took my message to heart and said, "Now that we have revisited the reasons why we have my portfolio invested the way we do, I agree we should stay the course and remain invested."

Sure enough, a few years later, he sent me a wonderful note. "Thank you for being there when I was in a lot of pain, and talking me through the whole strategy again. I am so glad I did not act on my own emotions."

I use that note whenever I need a reminder of why I'm doing this work. It's easy to be a coach or a point guard when things are going well. When a portfolio rises, it's easy to give someone an "atta boy." But I feel I become truly valuable when times are tough.

Wealth managers are trained to be unemotional and clear sighted, but I admit it's a lot easier for us because we aren't managing our own money—we are managing our clients' money. I completely understand how much harder it is for my clients to overcome their fears.

Of course, you are emotional about your money—your money means your future, even the futures of your children.

COUPLES AND THEIR FINANCIAL EMOTIONS

This dynamic may be even more dramatic when we are working with a couple. Sometimes one spouse focuses on finance and the other does not. But sometimes they disagree—with one spouse eager for more aggressive investments and the other saying, "I don't want to take any risk at all." At such moments, it's our job to be the *unemotional facilitator to a sensible solution.*

"Unfortunately," we might say, "taking no investment risk represents another kind of risk altogether. If you take no risk in your portfolio, you will receive little or no return on your investments. In that case, you won't be able to retire comfortably. Because we have created your long-term game plan, you can afford to take some *strategic risk* in your investment portfolio. By taking that risk, you will likely see much better rates of return, and you should be able to retire more comfortably."

We explain the effects of inflation, and how retirement income needs to grow over time. We explain to the more aggressive party how some wealth must be placed in conservative investments, especially for the early years of retirement.

When we put the discussion into a straightforward, logical framework, many spouses find it easier to come to an agreement. Sometimes that means meeting in the middle, at a level of risk both can accept.

Not to be sexist, but I find women to be better investors than men. I think women are better listeners, and they're more likely to heed advice. Men seem to be more focused on the here and now, while women seem more likely to think long term. Indeed, women tend to live longer than men, so women are more often put in the position of handling large sums of money alone. Recently, my brother wrote *What Now*, a book focused on the challenges faced by widows. Our firm is fortunate to work with and help many women overcome these challenges.

THE TRUE GOALS OF THE MEDIA

No one trades in fear like the media.

Truth be told, here in the United States we generally have far more good economic news than bad. But people don't watch the media for good news—why bother? You don't look over at the other side of the freeway if it's running freely. You look over when you see an accident. People will go two miles per hour in the hopes of seeing an injured soul hanging out a car window.

Human nature has us wired to be emotionally fixated on bad stuff. So, the media decides to keep on spewing "bad stuff" to get you to look.

It's crucial to remember that the financial media has two jobs, and neither of them has to do with the responsible assessment of financial markets. Their first job is to sell ads and their second job is to sell books. That's true if you are listening to the radio, the TV, or reading commentary on the Internet.

At this writing, one of the worst offenders is a fellow named Jim Cramer on CNBC. He is not a financial analyst, he is a book salesman. He sells his books through a kind of screaming flamboyance, and believe me, he sells a ton more books when he says things are looking bleak than when he says things are looking rosy.

Markets do not do well every year. Call it the 800-pound gorilla in the room. The truth everyone must confront.

But if you know the gorilla is standing right in front of you, you can plan around him. If you stare him right in the eye and *hold your ground,* you can relax and stop letting the media goad you into reacting every time he makes a move.

In the next chapter, I'll show you the wealth management consultative process I use as I start a relationship with a new client. Together we look risks straight in the eye and rationally assess goals.

Then I design a retirement game plan, which makes it much easier to ignore the media altogether.

CHAPTER 4

THE WEALTH MANAGEMENT CONSULTATIVE PROCESS

"If you don't know where you are going, any road will get you there."

—LEWIS CARROLL

In my firm, we don't just work with people nearing retirement, we work with folks in their thirties and early forties who want to make good financial decisions—and yes, eventually retire. Indeed, 70% of Americans between the ages of thirty and forty-nine rightly name retirement income as their biggest financial concern.[5] They realize

5 Source: Wealth2K, Inc.

that even though they may be socking away money in a 401(k) or another retirement savings account, building up a nest egg is very different than knowing how much income it will generate.

We do not, however, go straight to the bottom line. We follow a process to get to the bottom line. Good wealth management should never become a cookie-cutter process, but it must be a process. No two wealth management plans will be identical, but all good plans require a similar and highly -methodical approach...and a lot of questions.

THE DISCOVERY MEETING

"This above all: to thine own self be true,
And it must follow, as the night the day,
Thou canst not then be false to any man."

—SHAKESPEARE

When I head into the wealth management consultative process with a new client, I will ask upwards of sixty questions at our first discovery meeting. These questions go way beyond "what assets are you holding?" I want to understand people's values, their relationships, and their priorities.

It gets pretty personal. Who do you love? Do you want to leave money to your kids? If so, how much?

I will ask about your hobbies, about leasing vs. buying cars, about upcoming expenses like weddings and college, charitable inclinations, travel dreams—even about your pets. I don't do this for show. All this data goes into our system, and my staff records every single answer. My goal is to really understand what makes you tick.

I will also need to know about your other advisors, like lawyers, accountants, insurance agents, and existing financial planners. I will dive into your previous experiences with your team of advisors so I can help you evaluate them and recommend any missing players.

These meetings usually last about ninety minutes, and then I start to create your retirement game plan, based on the principles I will discuss in Chapters 5, 6, and 7.

Here's a diagram of the entire consultative process we follow here at the Marrella Group, kicked off by the discovery meeting. If your wealth manager cannot show you a similar, highly defined process, you should look elsewhere.

WEALTH MANAGMENT CONSULTATIVE PROCESS

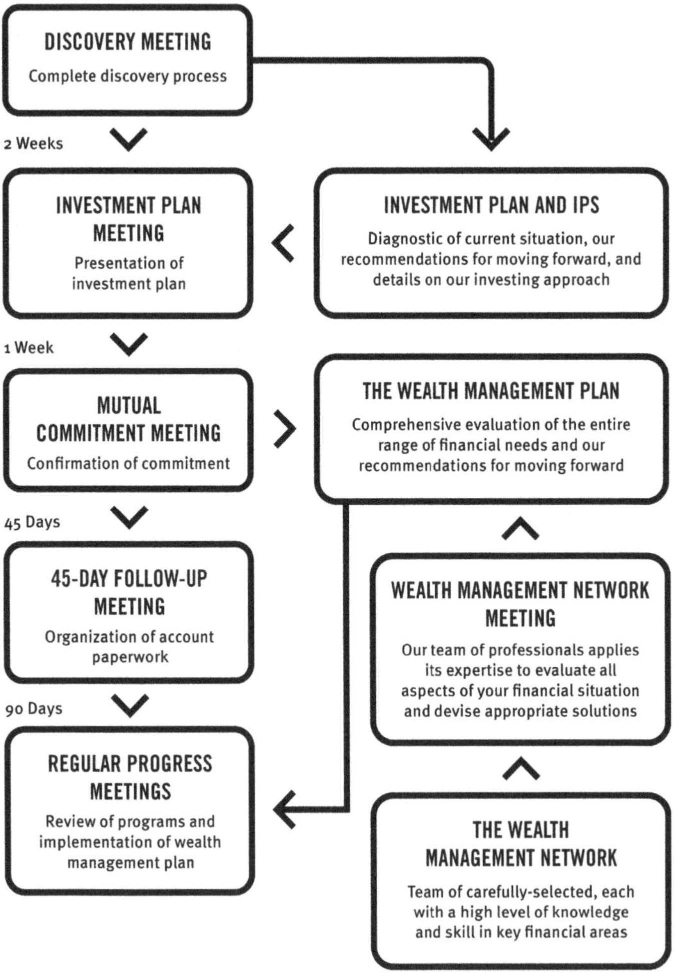
DISCOVERY MEETING
Complete discovery process
2 Weeks
INVESTMENT PLAN MEETING
Presentation of investment plan
INVESTMENT PLAN AND IPS
Diagnostic of current situation, our recommendations for moving forward, and details on our investing approach
1 Week
MUTUAL COMMITMENT MEETING
Confirmation of commitment
THE WEALTH MANAGEMENT PLAN
Comprehensive evaluation of the entire range of financial needs and our recommendations for moving forward
45 Days
45-DAY FOLLOW-UP MEETING
Organization of account paperwork
WEALTH MANAGEMENT NETWORK MEETING
Our team of professionals applies its expertise to evaluate all aspects of your financial situation and devise appropriate solutions
90 Days
REGULAR PROGRESS MEETINGS
Review of programs and implementation of wealth management plan
THE WEALTH MANAGEMENT NETWORK
Team of carefully-selected, each with a high level of knowledge and skill in key financial areas

GAME PLAN AND COMMITMENT

"Don't ever take a fence down until you know why it was put up."

—ROBERT FROST

After the discovery meeting, I step away for a couple of weeks to create your retirement game plan. First, I establish a target budget to fund your needs, wants, and dreams. Then I sit down and design an investment plan. The goal of this plan? Provide a thirty-plus year inflation-adjusted income stream. I lay out and discuss the strategy in great detail at a game plan meeting.

At that second meeting, you may feel compelled to say, "Let's do it!" But if that happens, I need to slow you down.

"Let's wait one more week," I'll say. "We'll set up another appointment and I'll have all the paperwork prepared and ready to go. This isn't something you should decide without careful consideration." If you are married, I'll ask you to go and discuss the game plan together, to make sure you are both comfortable moving forward.

Starting a new relationship with a wealth manager is a big deal. Often we are disrupting a relationship you have established with another financial advisor. We may be advising you to move out of certain investments to which you are emotionally attached. Some of these relationships and attachments may be strong and others not so strong, but we want to try to prevent buyer's remorse with this crucial cooling-off period.

Now that we know the details of your game plan, we will also discuss some of the pushback you might receive from your existing advisors and brokers. We know that once your current financial advisors find out what's transpiring, you will likely receive a phone call or two trying to talk you out of moving forward. We will go over the arguments you're likely to hear as others try to persuade you to change your mind.

And if you do change your mind? So be it. I think it is far better for you to change your mind up front, rather than after your accounts have been closed and transferred.

MUTUAL COMMITMENT

I call our third meeting the mutual commitment meeting. This is where you sign all of the necessary documents to open your new accounts, transfer your assets, and begin the creation of your retirement game plan.

Now you are a client, and your point guard has reported for duty!

At that meeting, I explain all the next steps and how they will lead up to the very important forty-five-day follow-up meeting.

THE FORTY-FIVE-DAY FOLLOW-UP

A lot has happened in the forty-five days following the mutual commitment meeting. My firm has set up your accounts, transferred your assets, and started implementing the strategies outlined in your game plan.

At the forty-five-day follow-up, I will go over all of the statements and other documents you have received in the mail. Honestly, you may have the feeling that we chopped down a large tree, sliced it into thin slices, and crammed them all into your mailbox. It may be overwhelming, but much of this paperwork is required by law. And much of it requires explanation. At the follow-up, I explain how to read your statements, and together we cull through what is important for you to keep.

At this meeting, I also typically introduce the rest of my staff and give my clients an overview of their online capabilities.

You will certainly have many questions, and this is

the meeting where you should get as many as possible answered.

REGULAR PROGRESS MEETINGS

After the big forty-five-day follow-up, we set up regular progress meetings every ninety days or so, depending on your situation and needs.

These progress meetings mean more than "checking in," because plenty has usually been happening behind the scenes. My firm has been working on the next phases of the game plan, like solving tax problems, establishing charitable funds, working on asset protection, and much more.

For example, we often find that clients don't have their estate planning documents in place, so we pro-actively set up an appointment with an estate attorney, and spend time talking about the issues and documents they need to bring to that attorney. By good advance prep, by the way, we can save them a lot of time and money.

WEALTH MANAGEMENT NETWORK MEETINGS

No wealth management firm can or should try to do it all themselves. I mentioned how we sometimes try to meld with a client's existing team of accountants, lawyers, etc., and how we sometimes bring in people we trust from our own network. In either case, constant communications and the occasional meetings with network professionals are crucial to keeping any game plan on track.

We schedule these encounters as part of regular progress meetings or, of course, as needed. Any firm you look at should be able to show you how they connect to other professionals and bring them in to help.

MORE ABOUT COMMITMENT

Sometimes clients will come to us and say, "I'm not interested in a game plan. I'm not interested in wealth management. I would just like to give you this $1 million and see how much money you can make for me."

As true wealth managers, however, we are just not interested in relationships like that. We are only interested in working with people for whom we can have a long-term impact. Otherwise, we will be judged only on a quarterly investment return—and that doesn't lead to long-term relationships.

To use a sports analogy, suppose Joe Montana, the famous quarterback, had been judged only on one bad game in which he threw several interceptions. Joe Montana is not in the Hall of Fame based on a single game, but on an entire career of work—a career that made a huge difference for his teams. Like your overall retirement plan, we never want to be judged on the outcome of a single investment.

YES, SHE COULD RETIRE

"You can't win unless you try to win, but you can lose by trying not to lose."

—JACK CAMPBELL

Let me give you an example of the consultative process in action. This time, it was a happy process indeed. You see, unlike Bill at the oil company, whom we met in the Introduction, Maryanne was able to retire young.

She just didn't know it when she walked in our door.

Maryanne was in her late fifties and still working hard as an insurance adjuster. Her husband Jack was a cancer survivor. Jack was now in remission and doing well, but the illness had changed his perspective on life and he had retired early. Jack was worried that his cancer might recur, and he had a lot of anxiety around the fact that his wife was still working. Not knowing how many years they had left to enjoy together, he really wanted her to retire as soon as possible.

At sixty-three, Jack was a bit older than Maryanne, and if full retirement for both of them didn't work out, he wasn't sure he would be able to re-enter the workforce at anywhere near his previous salary level.

At Jack's urging, Maryanne had scheduled her own retirement with her employer *no less than three times*, but had backed out each time. Why? Every time she got close to a retirement date, something would happen in the news. She'd see distress on Wall Street, she'd hear the noise in the media get louder and louder, and then she'd get spooked.

Maryanne was lucky to have some pension income, but she was too young for Social Security. She and Jack had saved about $1.1 million over the years by giving up luxuries—money they had instead placed into solid investments.

They had a nice nest egg, but was it really enough to retire so young? After all, the younger you retire, the higher your risk of running out of money. Maryanne understood completely that she needed to think about *income* rather than savings, but how could the math work, exactly? How could their nest egg be translated into a retirement income stream to carry her and Jack through the three great risks of timing, inflation, and longevity? Both Maryanne's parents were in their late eighties, so she knew she herself was likely to live pretty long.

In addition, Jack and Maryanne still had two kids in college.

We sat down and put together a thirty-plus year plan: Social Security income, pension income, and investment income. We looked at their lifestyle costs and the money they had already set aside in a college fund. And guess what? In their case, we only needed to allocate about $600,000 of their $1.1 million portfolio to generate the necessary income streams to cover them into their nineties. That left about $500,000 for extras, like emergencies, special trips, a legacy for the kids, you name it (in Chapter 6, you'll see that this money went into the "safety segment").

When I presented their retirement game plan, Jack and Maryanne glowed. They saw in cold hard numbers that yes, indeed, they had enough money to restructure their investments into a conservatively built retirement income plan with a half-million dollars in reserve. We went over a precise thirty-plus-year road map and I explained how it addressed the three great risks.

The result? Mystery and uncertainty evaporated. Jack and Maryanne learned they could stop following CNBC in fear. In fact, they could stop following CNBC altogether. She called human resources the next day to schedule her retirement for the fourth and final time.

CHAPTER 5

INCOME GOAL SETTING AND MONITORING

"The greater danger for most of us lies not in setting our aim too high and falling short; but in setting our aim too low, and achieving our mark."

—MICHELANGELO

How do you know what's going to happen to your money over thirty-plus years, given that the market will have its ups and downs and you will be drawing income all along the way?

The answer, of course, is that you cannot know—except within degrees of probability. Thanks to modern computer software, however, those probabilities can at least be estimated.

Most investment counselors specializing in retirement now follow a standard procedure for dealing with the future impact of market volatility and timing risk. We call our process Goal Planning and Monitoring (GPM). This process employs a sophisticated software tool that calculates your probability of success by using different market rates of return and volatility variables to create projections of potential portfolio outcomes.

We call these "Monte Carlo simulation trials."

In general, investment returns simulated by Monte Carlo trials yield wildly diverse results, including some with huge losses and others with huge gains, depending on different market scenarios.

I find GPM useful, but I know it clearly doesn't tell the whole story or solve the whole problem. For example, the tool defines the confidence zone as a 75% or better outcome of the GPM. In other words, a 75% chance of you still having money in the bank when you pass away.

Unfortunately, most investment counselors stop after running this software and say, "Look, according to this software model, the results indicate that you have a 75% chance of success and you are in the confidence zone!"

At that point, you may be forgiven for asking, "What about that other 25% probability?"

Let's take a look at one of these software models, in which a series of investments are launched in year one. Then a thousand different potential market scenarios are analyzed over your projected retirement.

TOM AND MARY IN MONTE CARLO

"For all of its uncertainty, we cannot flee the future."

—BARBARA JORDAN

Tom and Mary, both age sixty-four, are preparing to retire. Once they look at their budget, they set a goal of living on $5,000 a month, or $60,000 a year, plus healthcare expenses. The tool includes a built-in assumption of 6.5% in healthcare inflation.

Along with their Social Security incomes, Tom and Mary are starting out their retirement with $1.4 million in investments. Right off, the tool tells us that if Tom and Mary were able to achieve a consistent 4.5% rate of return for the rest of their lives, they would have a 100% chance of achieving their inflation-adjusted goal.

But what if something else happens?

In the charted example,[6] the GPM software has run 1,000 Monte Carlo trials using different market volatility and rate of return assumptions on Tom and Mary's portfolio. You will see a linear 4.5% return for the thirty-year period, represented by the thick black line. Under this "average" scenario, they have done better than not run out of money, they still have $863,000 left at the end of the day. As you look at this line, however, it's important to remember that returns are not linear. Interest rates change and market returns change. Tom and Mary may average a 4.5% return over thirty years, yet not once earn 4.5% in any single year.

Overall, the GPM measures the vast differences in the 1,000 different sequences of Tom and Mary's returns. Other scenarios, tracked by the gray lines across time, turn out better or worse. The dotted line shows another possible end point of $375,000 left when they both pass away. That's a "bad timing line" of market returns, but Tom and Mary are still doing fine.

You can see that given a standard investment scheme, Tom and Mary will realize an astounding difference in possible outcomes—including a huge $5 million difference between the worst and best scenarios.

6 The images [and/or screenshots] are reproduced from the Goal Planning & Monitoring financial planning software, ©PIEtech, Inc. Used with permission. All rights reserved.

Tom and Mary could die rich or they could die broke. But the important question should be, "Will they run out of money before they die?"

INSIDE THE NUMBERS: 1000 TRIALS

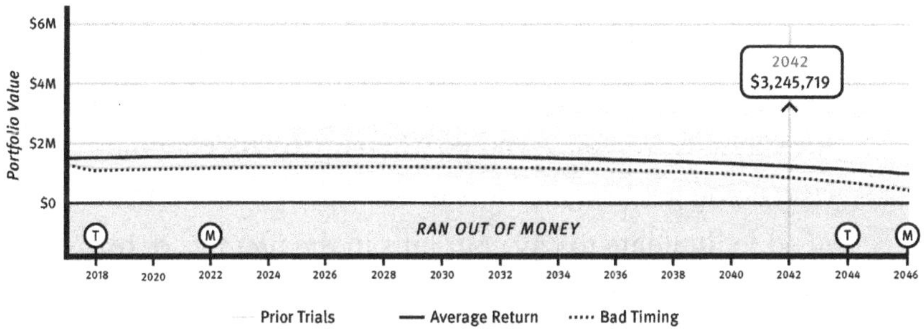

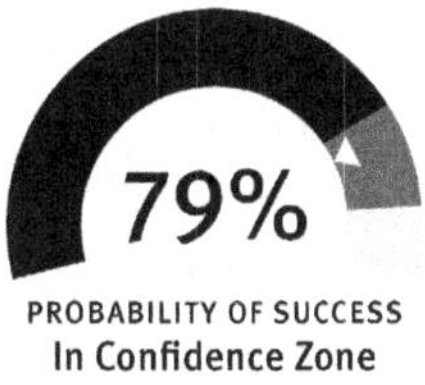

This graph shows the results for all 1000 Monte Carlo Trials. The Probability of Success meter displays the percentage of trials that were successful in funding all of your goals. We identify the Confidence Zone as a probability of success between 75% and 90%.

In this model, the software has come up with a 79% chance that Tom and Mary will meet their inflation-adjusted goal of $5,000 a month (aside from healthcare expenses) for the rest of their lives.

The software puts them in the confidence zone—but of course, that means they have a 21% chance of running out of money altogether. Or, looking at the chart, 21% of the Monte Carlo probability lines bottoming out at zero before the game is over.

Anyone who studies these models and runs a series of Monte Carlo trials quickly realizes that *market volatility in the early years of retirement matters a great deal more* than the volatility later on. As noted when we discussed timing risk, if you get lousy returns in the early years, and you need to liquidate to pay your bills in the first five or ten years of your retirement—the later results will certainly be worse.

75% ISN'T THRILLING

Some days, I may have four different couples come into my office to talk about their retirement situations. Before I created the retirement game plan, if I ran a GPM for these couples and their results came in at a 75% probability of success, I too would tell them the software had put them in the confidence zone.

But a 75% chance of success, even a 79% chance, as shown for Tom and Mary, never seemed enough to me. That meant one out of those four couples could run out of money. Would a dentist be happy if one out of four of his patients lost their teeth? I am guessing no way. I know for sure I would not be remembered as a great wealth manager if one out of four of my clients ran out of money.

So, I started looking for an investment methodology that would not depend on any algorithms I didn't fully understand. Nor would I settle for a confidence zone that starts at only 75%.

In *Your Retirement Game Plan,* I'm shooting for 100% certainty—or as close as humanly possible. I know I can only head toward 100% by controlling the three great risks, and the emotional risk too.

Let's look at how the right game plan raises your odds.

CHAPTER 6

A SEGMENTED RETIREMENT INCOME PLAN

"Planning is bringing the future into the present so that you can do something about it now"

—ALAN LAKEIN

Every one of my clients may be different, but at the heart of every retirement game plan I build lives a segmented retirement income strategy. I know of no other better way to create thirty-plus years of confidence, with or without a pension.

In this chapter, I'll lay out the concept and, in the next, I'll give you a realistic case study.[7]

7 This and other examples are hypothetical, and are not indicative of any specific situation. Future performance cannot be guaranteed and investment yields will fluctuate with market conditions.

SIX SEGMENTS PLUS

In the income segmentation strategy, your savings are invested *up front* into six very different time segments designed specifically to address the timing, inflation, and longevity risks. In addition, money is set aside for a safety segment.

Think of a timeline which runs from zero–thirty-plus years, beginning on the day you retire, with segments covering each five years. To protect against timing and emotional risks, investments in each segment are *totally dedicated to those specific years in advance,* and must not be touched until their time has come.

SEGMENTED INVESTMENT GAME PLAN

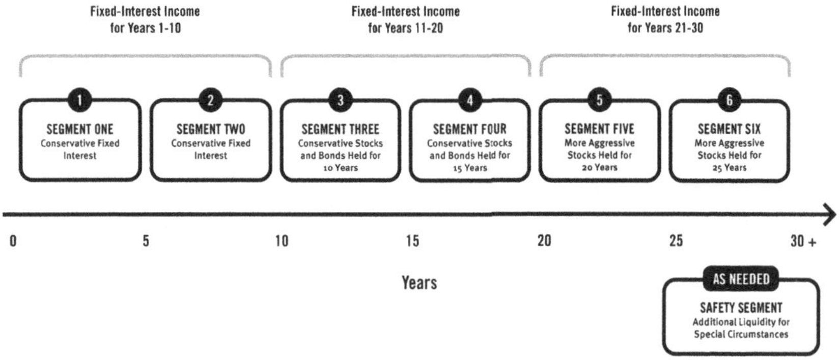

SEGMENT ONE: YEARS 1–5

Remember that the most critical mistakes usually come in the early years of retirement. For that reason, Segment One, which covers the first five years, is invested conservatively in safe, income-generating financial vehicles. The rate of return on these safe vehicles may be low, but the rate must be secondary to the safety and the predictability of the underlying investment.

Why? Because Segment One has only one job: to pay you monthly income for the first sixty months of your retirement.

If stocks should tumble two years into your game plan, your monthly paycheck will not be at risk. You can ride out any financial storm because you still have three years of predictable income to count on.

You can think of Segment One as an anchor for your emotions as you head into retirement. You can then spend the monthly income it produces with confidence, because *Segment One has no need to survive beyond those sixty months* to support your later years. Other segments will do that job.

EARLY YEARS OF RETIREMENT: TIMING RISK MOST DANGEROUS

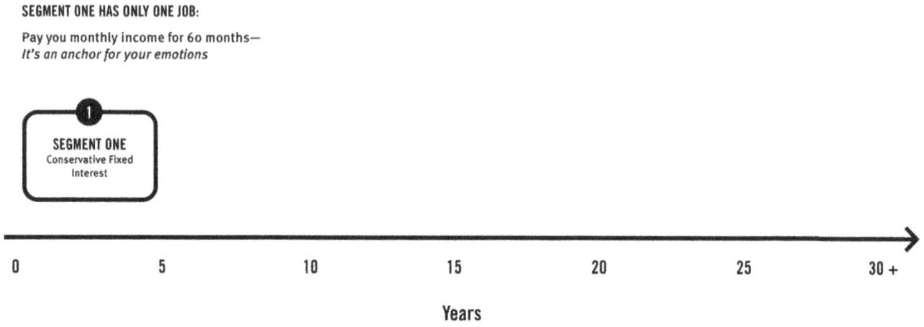
SEGMENT ONE HAS ONLY ONE JOB:
Pay you monthly income for 60 months—
It's an anchor for your emotions
1
SEGMENT ONE
Conservative Fixed Interest
0
5
10
15
20
25
30 +
Years

SEGMENT TWO: YEARS 6–10

What happens after that first five years, even if Segment One has been completely exhausted?

Now you turn to your Segment Two money, which was also invested conservatively, back at the beginning of your retirement. During those first five years, while you were living off Segment One, Segment Two was quietly accumulating and earning a reliable, fixed rate of interest. Now, beginning in year six, Segment Two takes over.

EARLY YEARS OF RETIREMENT: TIMING RISK MOST DANGEROUS

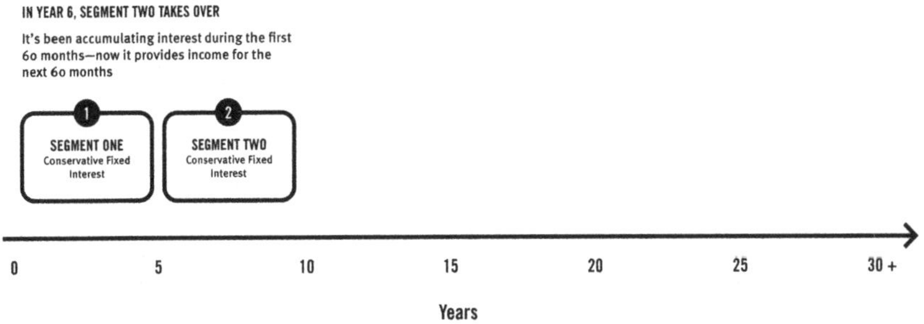
IN YEAR 6, SEGMENT TWO TAKES OVER
It's been accumulating interest during the first 60 months—now it provides income for the next 60 months
1
SEGMENT ONE
Conservative Fixed Interest
2
SEGMENT TWO
Conservative Fixed Interest
0
5
10
15
20
25
30 +
Years

Segment Two also has one job and one job only. It must provide you an additional sixty months of predictable monthly income. The income should be higher in Segment Two, which is important as it needs to keep you up with inflation. Why will it be higher? The money you left untouched and accumulating in Segment Two should have grown.

Together, Segments One and Two produce monthly income for the first ten years of retirement, regardless of market conditions, and without endangering your investment for years eleven to thirty-plus.

Now you have effectively addressed the risk of retiring in a bad year.

EARLY YEARS OF RETIREMENT: TIMING RISK MOST DANGEROUS

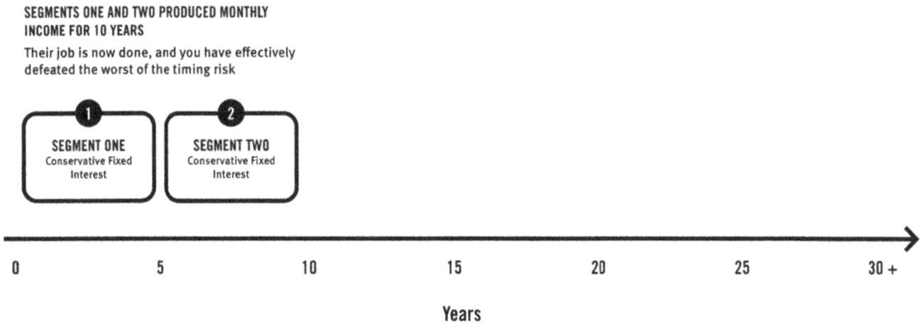
SEGMENTS ONE AND TWO PRODUCED MONTHLY INCOME FOR 10 YEARS
Their job is now done, and you have effectively defeated the worst of the timing risk
1
SEGMENT ONE
Conservative Fixed Interest
2
SEGMENT TWO
Conservative Fixed Interest
0
5
10
15
20
25
30 +
Years

SEGMENTS THREE AND FOUR: YEARS 11–20

As we move into Segment Three, a decade past your initial retirement, we turn our attention from the timing risk to the inflation risk. I hope I don't have to repeat my warnings about the reality of inflation. Let me just say here that if you're close to retirement, some of you will remember paying less for your first house than your latest car.

To keep pace with inflation, we need a portion of our longer-term investments to rest in stocks. Stocks are riskier. Investments in stocks are not a sure thing like the conservative vehicles we utilized in Segments One and Two; and, as they say in every financial statement, "past results are no guarantee of future results." But it's also true that stocks have outpaced inflation over time.

In general, I recommend that 50% of the investments for Segments Three and Four be placed in stocks and 50% in bonds. The basket of stocks will be relatively conservative, but we will be trusting that these equities will produce returns beating both inflation and the fixed-interest rates we could have received in safer vehicles.

MIDDLE YEARS: INFLATION RISK

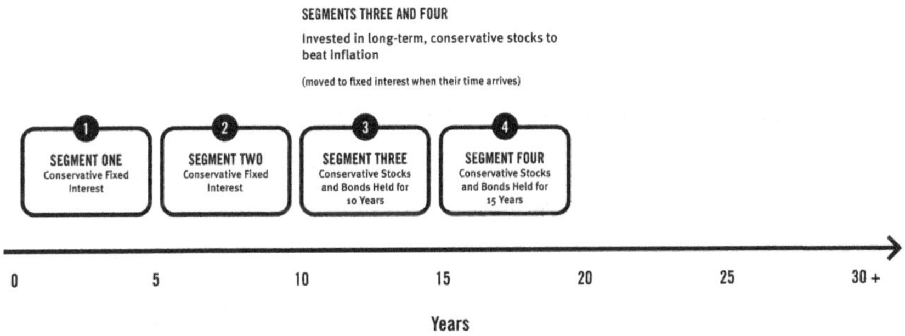

MOVING MONEY TO FIXED-INTEREST VEHICLES AS A SEGMENT KICKS IN

What happens when it comes time to move on to the next segment on our timeline?

Prior to the year when you need to access Segments Three, Four, Five, or Six to produce income, *all* the investments from that segment will be moved into a more conservative, interest-earning investment vehicle. Why? To make sure that the returns for each of those next five years are as safe and predictable as those early segments.

Moving money out of stocks into safer vehicles at the beginning of each segment is a key principle of the game plan. If you know your monthly income for the next five years will be stable, you will find it far easier to control your emotions and stick with the plan.

Remember: You never need to risk the money in any one segment to fund a later segment, and you must not be tempted to do so. Each of the six segments has its own job, and that job is to fund a five-year period. That's it. No segment must be cannibalized to support another segment.

ADDRESSING LONGEVITY AND LIQUIDITY

Together, Segments Five and Six address the longevity risk.

You need to plan for the possibility that you do in fact see a thirty-plus year retirement. The last years may be your least active, and require less money for travel and recreation, but you will still need ample income. Healthcare and homecare costs may become a much larger part of your budget, regardless of your insurance coverage.

For Segments Five and Six, we may be placing *all* of our investment in stocks and taking somewhat more risk. But it is a well-calculated risk.

Statistics show that in 1949 through 2012, large-cap stocks produced higher average returns that were significantly higher than inflation *in 100% of twenty-year rolling periods.* That means if you put money into a diverse mixture of large-cap stocks in *any year between 1949 and 2012, and waited a full twenty years,* you would have beaten inflation.

In other words, if you can wait twenty years, a well-managed stock portfolio should pay off nicely.

LATER YEARS: LONGEVITY RISK

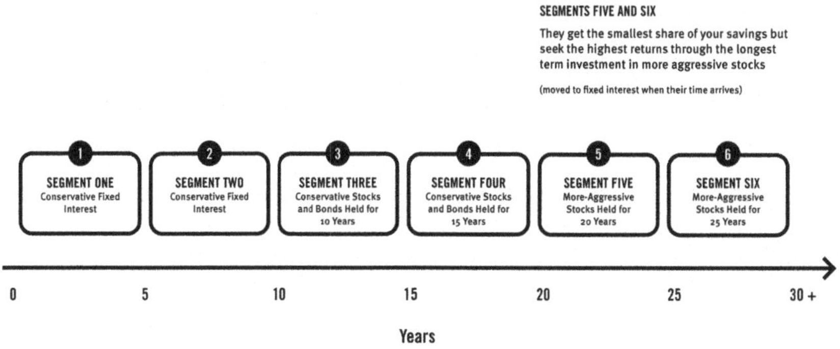

To better understand this strategy, you must make the transition to thinking in "sequential" returns rather than "linear" returns. For example, in the Goal Setting and Monitoring discussion of the last chapter, we looked at a 4.5% average return line over twenty-five years. But in truth, that represented not a linear set of returns, but a set of sequences in which Tom and Mary may have averaged 6% and 8% losses in years one and two, offset by 18% and 20% gains in the last two years, to bring the overall average to 4.5%.

You must give your segments their proper time—and you must not assume that whatever is happening this year will happen next year.

For the plan to work, however, you must stick with the investments within your segments. The four five-year segments from years eleven to thirty hold an allocation of stocks designed to be held for increasingly longer periods. These segments, held for the longest period, generally receive the smallest share of your initial savings, but they are also the segments that seek the highest returns.

If you place $100,000 in Segment Five for twenty years and receive a 2% average rate of return over those twenty years, your $100,000 will grow to $148,000 by the time you move it into a conservative vehicle for its five-year job. At a 4% average rate of return, it will have grown to $219,000. At 6%, it will have grown to $320,000.

Because we have time to absorb the volatility, it's actually *more prudent* to invest this longer-term money *more aggressively* than *safely*.

In our practice, we typically utilize two distinctly different mutual fund portfolios for long-term growth. The first portfolio employs active management and the second is managed passively. We do this because active managers sometimes outdo passive managers—and sometimes vice versa. Using both allows for a portfolio that is even more diversified.

ADJUSTING AT SEGMENT FIVE

As you move into Segment Five, you will likely be in your eighties. At this point, we will likely have a lot more information about your longevity and spending needs. As is true throughout your plan, we are always monitoring to see if it makes sense to make any adjustments.

For example, you may not have spent all of the income provided in previous segments, or the investments in Segments Five and Six may have significantly outperformed our modest expectations. In both cases, we may transition more quickly out of the stock portfolios into more conservative vehicles to reduce our exposure to volatility of the market.

Such decisions are done on an individual basis, and are somewhat beyond the scope of this book.

THE SAFETY SEGMENT

In addition to the six segments, we need to create an entirely different portfolio. This fund will protect against a potentially longer life, but also provides additional liquidity.

I call this fund the Safety Segment, and it will be earmarked for additional personal goals, special situations, as well as family emergencies that may arise along the road.

It may be that come year ten, you have the chance to sail around the world with friends. Or take the extended family to Cancun for your fiftieth anniversary. You know you *cannot touch the money in any other segment* to fund that amazing life opportunity. So you tap into your Safety Segment.

Liquidity is important for these opportunities, but also for some financial flexibility. It may be that in years eighteen to nineteen, you will want to move some money into cash so that you don't have to pull your long-term investment in Segment Five if you face some financial difficulties. It's likely that your Safety Segment will be worth a bundle by then, so it can provide a "bridge loan" to Segment Five as stocks recover.

Here's the full picture, once again:

SIX SEGMENTS PLUS THE SAFETY SEGMENT

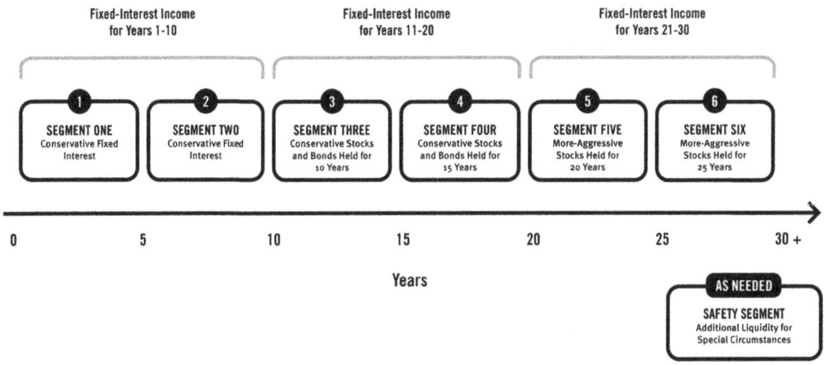

HOW MUCH IN EACH SEGMENT?

"In life, most short cuts end up taking longer than taking the longer route."

—SUZY KASSEM

How much money should you designate for each segment?

If a couple like Tom and Mary from Chapter 5 had $1.4 million in investable funds on the day they retired, and they had "typical needs," I would put $882,000 across Segments Two through Six, and the rest in the Safety Segment. Here's how I would divide up their $1.4 million in year zero:

- Segment One: $165,792
- Segment Two: $179,464

- Segment Three: $163,799
- Segment Four: $162,799
- Segment Five: $110,489
- Segment Six: $ 99,446
- Safety Segment: $518,000

Notice again that the lowest allocations go to the long-term investments in Segments Five and Six.

Of course, depending on how much money this couple has relative to their needs, and the answers I get during the discovery phase of our consultation, I might suggest different investment strategies from a typical profile. For this reason alone, I do not think anyone should attempt to do this math themselves—and I must caution you that segmentation *cannot be planned outside of the holistic wealth management process* I described in Chapter 2.

A well-crafted retirement game plan will build a segmented investment strategy that is highly customized: What other income streams do you have? Are you expecting an inheritance? Do you think it's important to leave a financial legacy to your children? Can you foresee extraordinary expenses? Do you have a medical condition that might limit your overall life expectancy? Do you have a dream you want to fulfill?

Budgeting for expected lifestyle changes will also play a factor. For many people, retirement divides into three overall phases, which might be nicknamed *go-go, slow-go, and no-go,* each lasting about ten years. (My apologies for the "no-go" nickname, but I couldn't resist the rhyme.)

In other words, your highest activity years will likely come at the beginning of your retirement, followed by a period of slowing down, followed by a period of highly reduced recreational expenses.

These questions and assumptions must be factored into your personal game plan. There are no short cuts.

CHAPTER 7

CASE STUDY: JACK AND JANE

"Retirement is when you stop living at work and begin working at living."

—ANONYMOUS

Now that you have a basic understanding of the income segmentation strategy underlying your retirement game plan, let's create a more detailed case study, this time for a very nice couple we'll call Jack and Jane.

Jack and Jane are both sixty-five and looking to retire this year—if they can do so with confidence. They've worked hard their whole lives. Each will be receiving some Social Security income, but neither one has a pension. These folks are pretty fit and very healthy, so they're looking forward to a long and active life together.

In my first meeting with Jack and Jane, I explained all about *holistic wealth management* using the chalkboard algebra in Chapter 2. Then I kicked off the consultative process by asking all those important questions we talked about in Chapter 3. We discussed their housing costs, travel goals, and many other factors. They mentioned they'd like to take their grandkids on some trips. And they wanted to make sure they have a little extra cash to help out their kids from time to time.

Whatever decisions we make together, we want to make sure those decisions are made in light of all their goals and challenges.

Jack expects $30,000 a year in Social Security income, with an expected annual increase of 2%. Jane expects $15,000 a year in Social Security, also expected to increase by about 2% a year due to cost-of-living increases.

When it comes to assets, Jack and Jane did a little better than Tom and Mary. They've managed to sock away $2 million earmarked for their retirement. The money's already invested, but it's liquid and easy to redeploy.

After our initial meeting, my staff and I analyzed their responses. After that, we deployed our analytic tools to build out the financial models we needed to create their plan. Then I invited Jack and Jane back in to present the strategy that would allow them to retire with confidence and peace of mind: their complete retirement game plan.

At the heart of that plan was the investment segmentation approach we learned about in Chapter 6.

LOOKING FOR $90,000 A YEAR

"Annual income twenty pounds, annual expenditure nineteen six, result happiness. Annual income twenty pounds, annual expenditure twenty pound ought and six, result misery."

—CHARLES DICKENS, *DAVID COPPERFIELD*

According to everything we've learned, we figure that Jack and Jane will need about $90,000 a year, adjusted for inflation, to achieve their hoped-for lifestyle. That's $7,500 a month in today's dollars for the next thirty-plus years.

Of course, the $90,000 figure only represents an average, because life never works out quite so neatly. Indeed, I imagine that, like most couples, Jack and Jane will enjoy having more income in their early years and will likely require less in their latter years—in accordance with the typical "go-go, slow-go, and no-go" phases of retirement.

LAYING IT OUT FOR JACK AND JANE

Now we've come to our second meeting, and Jack and Jane have settled into the conference room. I set up my PowerPoint projector and drop a couple of binders on the table.

For the rest of this chapter I'll just pretend that you, my readers, are Jack and Jane. That way, I can tell you more directly how the income plan works.

So, Jack and Jane, I say after the coffee arrives, I have created a retirement income plan for you by utilizing two different tools—one rather simple and the second more complex.

The first tool provides Goal Planning and Monitoring. I input your goals and objectives, your two Social Security incomes, as well as the predicted average income from your $2 million portfolio. Here's a breakout of your current assets:

JACK & JANE'S INVESTMENT ASSETS SUMMARY		
Asset	Owner	Current Value
Jack's Traditional IRA	Jack	$500,000
Jane's Traditional IRA	Jane	$500,000
Joint Investment Account	Joint Survivorship	$750,000
Savings	Joint Survivorship	$250,000
TOTAL OF ALL ASSETS		**$2,000,000**

Your Social Security streams add up to just $45,000 a year, or $3,750 a month in today's dollars, with an expected 2% annual increase.

That means we need a strategy, using your investment portfolio, to make up the difference and get you to the $7,500 you need.

JACK & JANE'S MONTE CARLO TRIALS

Without any additional planning, if you simply place that money into traditional, diversified vehicles and start pulling cash, we'd be looking at a wide range of Monte Carlo trials over three decades.

This tool[8] ran 1,000 different market scenarios, and all those little gray lines represent the probabilities of you

8 The images [and/or screenshots] are reproduced from the Goal Planning & Monitoring financial planning software, ©PIEtech, Inc. Used with permission. All rights reserved.

running out of money or ending up with money in the bank over the course of time—given your desire to take out $90,000 a year in today's dollars over thirty years of retirement.

You can see that in the very best scenario, you ended up with an amazing $7 million after thirty years. But that would mean a lot of luck both in the economy and in the markets. In the worst trial, you ran out of money in about seventeen years.

INSIDE THE NUMBERS: 1000 TRIALS

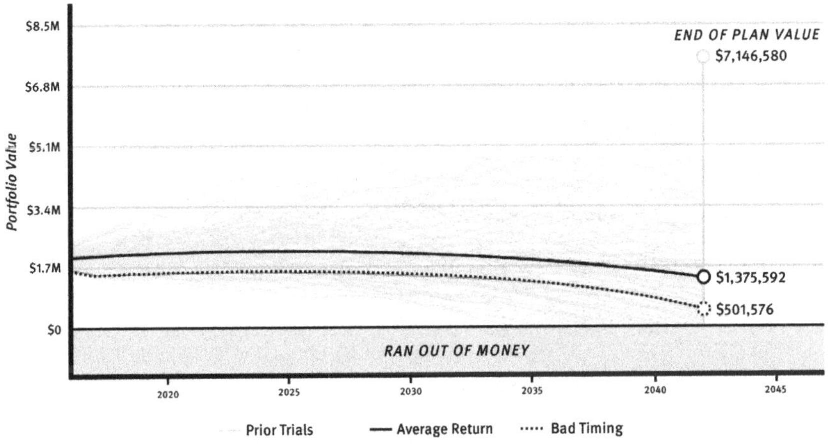

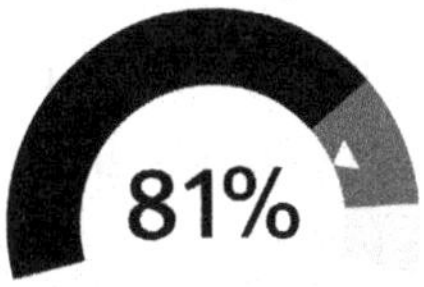

PROBABILITY OF SUCCESS
In Confidence Zone

This graph shows the results for all 1000 Monte Carlo Trials. The Probability of Success meter displays the percentage of trials that were successful in funding all of your goals. We identify the Confidence Zone as a probability of success between 75% and 90%.

The thick dotted line indicates "bad market timing" for your initial retirement investments. In other words, if you retire at a bad time, and your portfolio sustains losses or low rates of return early on in your retirement, it's likely to lead to undesirable outcomes. One of the risks I hope to offset is the chance of you retiring at a bad time and getting adverse rates of return early on.

The thick, continuous line shows an average projected rate of return of 4.95%. If you were to get 4.95% each and every year, you would have a 100% chance of success, and you would pass away with $1.375 million still left in your portfolio. So staying on that thick continuous line would be just great.

Unfortunately, the real world cannot be so easily predicted, especially over thirty years.

WHAT ABOUT THOSE RISKS?

What is this Monte Carlo tool really telling you? Remember the three risks we talked about earlier? Longevity, inflation, and timing? This tool helps us decide whether you are in a position to retire safely, relative to those risks.

This analysis represents a thirty-year timeframe, so it's giving us a clear sense of the longevity risk. It takes you out until age ninety-five. And the tool has a built-in 3% inflation rate, so we're also addressing the inflation risk.

But with respect to timing risk, it indicates that you would run out of money 19% of the time. That puts you firmly inside the tool's definition of the confidence zone. Honestly, that's not too bad—but I don't think it's good enough. If you retire today and today turns out to be really bad timing in the markets, your retirement lifestyle could be in jeopardy. You deserve better.

To make sure you can really relax and enjoy your retirement, I've created a more sophisticated model for *Your Retirement Game Plan*. To design this model, I'm using a second analytical tool.

JACK AND JANE'S SEGMENTED PLAN

"Happiness is not the absence of problems, it's the ability to deal with them."

—STEVE MARABOLI

Within this second tool, I've broken the next thirty years into six five-year segments, with different investments and income streams planned for each segment of your retirement. Let's start with the first two segments, covering the first ten years.

THE GO-GO YEARS

We talked about an average $7,500 a month, or $90,000 a year over the course of your retirement. But because you are both healthy, active people, I think a better plan will provide more income in the first ten years, in what I call the "go-go" phase. Over these first ten years, you'll likely have more opportunities to travel and do more things that will require more money.

So, in the first ten years, I've structured a plan to give you $100,000 a year, or $8,333 a month of income in today's dollars. In order to get there, I'm advising you to immediately place two separate blocks of initial investments into very safe vehicles: $274,980 to generate income for the first five years, and $285,241 to generate income for the second five years. Here's the full breakout for Segments 1 and 2:

	SEGMENT 1	SEGMENT 2
Years	1-5	6-10
Income Duration	5 Years	5 Years
Income Start Year	1	6
Monthly Income in Today's Dollars	$8,333	$8,333
Inflation-Adjusted Income	$8,333	$9,660
Deferral Rate of Return	N/A	2.00%
Withdrawal Rate of Return	0.00%	2.00%
Segment Starting Value	$274,980	$285,241

In this and the following charts, the numbers break out like this:

Income Duration: How long the money in each segment needs to generate inflation-adjusted income.

Income Start Year: The first year each segment needs to begin delivering monthly income to the retiree.

Deferral Duration: The amount of time the money in each segment lies completely untouched, growing in value until its income start year.

Monthly Income in Today's Dollars: The amount of monthly income that will be used by the retiree beginning in the income start year, expressed in today's dollars. The actual dollars will increase with inflation, but the value is expressed in today's money. The monthly income will come from a combination of Social Security and withdrawals from the appropriate segment accounts.

Inflation-Adjusted Income: Anticipated actual dollars, given an assumed 3% rate of inflation. Just remember these dollars are worth less than today's dollars, so it's really the "Today's Dollars" column that counts.

Deferral Rate of Return: The rate of return needed during the deferred "waiting" years in order for the segment money to grow sufficiently to produce the needed retiree income beginning in the income start year. I've used very realistic, conservative numbers.

Withdrawal Rate of Return: The rate of return needed

during the five years of withdrawal in order for the segment money to provide the needed retiree income. Again, we're assuming a very conservative return. Just to play it really safe, we're assuming you will get a 0% rate of return during the withdrawal of Segment 1 funds.

Segment Starting Value: The amount of money in today's dollars placed in the segment at the very beginning of the game plan.

As you enter each segment's first year, you will begin drawing money out of these investments to supplement your Social Security and keep yourself at $8,333 a month—making sure you never touch the money slated for later years. In the later segments, that will mean moving the money out of stocks and into CDs and other safe accounts.

THE SLOW-GO YEARS

As we move into year eleven of your retirement, when you're in your mid-seventies, I'm expecting you to slow down a little in activity and reduce your need for income. Let's call this next decade the slow-go years. At this point, I'm expecting you to be comfortable dropping back to our overall average goal of $90,000 a year—adjusted for inflation.

I'm going to have you invest $233,827 right now into investments designed to yield the necessary returns ten years from now, when you enter year eleven. In that year, you'll redeploy this money into completely safe income-bearing accounts to get you through those next five years.

For Segment 4, intended for years sixteen to twenty, I'm going to have you invest $243,081 in the same way as Segment 3: accounts with stable and predictable returns. When you enter year sixteen, you'll transition that money into safe interest-bearing accounts to get you through years sixteen to twenty.

	SEGMENT 3	SEGMENT 4
Years	11-15	16-20
Income Duration	5 years	5 Years
Income Start Year	11	16
Monthly Income in Today's Dollars	$7,500	$7,500
Inflation-Adjusted Income	$10,079	$11,685
Deferral Rate of Return	3.00%	3.00%
Withdrawal Rate of Return	2.00%	2.00%
Segment Starting Value	$233,827	$243,081

As you can see, the monies earmarked for Segments 3 and 4 are also invested very conservatively. They're only required to earn 3% in order to provide the necessary income. It's important for the first twenty years of your income to be derived from very safe investments. This helps create the confidence you are looking for.

Let me just remind you again that with all these charts and numbers, you have to keep in mind that every single figure must be adjusted for inflation. In all my software models, inflation has been pegged at 3% on average each year. Three percent sounds small, but it adds up to a lot over ten or twenty years. When we look at Segment 3, where it says $7,500 in today's dollars, that inflation-adjusted number is actually $10,079.

With inflation, and based on this software model, you will indeed have $10,079 a month available to you at that point in time—but its buying power will be the same as $7,500 in today's money.

I should point out that many models do not take inflation properly into account. So be careful when you make comparisons to other investment strategies.

YEARS TWENTY-ONE AND BEYOND

When you reach years twenty-one and beyond, both of you will be in your mid-eighties. Realistically, you are likely to need yet less income because you'll probably be traveling a good deal less and dropping out of some other expensive activities. Let's call these the no-go years, and dedicate somewhat less income to these years.

I really don't like the term "no-go," but it just fits so nicely with "go-go" and "slow-go" that I allow it into my vernacular. If "a little slower than slow-go" rhymed, I would gladly use that term instead. Perhaps you will be climbing Mt. Everest at eighty-five.

Don't worry, you'll still have plenty of income, just a little bit less than before.

I'm going to have you invest $125,787 of your current nest egg into Segment 5, targeted for years twenty-one to twenty-five. That money will be more aggressively invested into stocks, and designed to grow at an average of 6% over the next twenty years. That way, when you near year twenty-one, you can transition that chunk of money, moving it into safer interest-bearing vehicles, and enjoy it for years twenty-one to twenty-five.

I'm also going to advise you to invest another $113,031 into stocks earmarked to fund Segment 6 for years twenty-six to thirty, when you folks have hit your early nineties. That $113,031 will likely have grown substantially over the course of twenty-five years. Like the previous segments, this block of money will find its way into safer investments just prior to year twenty-six, so that you can enjoy yet another predictable stream of five-year, inflation-adjusted income.

	SEGMENT 5	SEGMENT 6
Years	21-25	26-30
Income Duration	5 Years	5 Years
Income Start Year	21	26
Monthly Income in Today's Dollars	$7,000	$7,000
Inflation-Adjusted Income	$12,643	$14,656
Deferral Rate of Return	6.00%	6.00%
Withdrawal Rate of Return	2.00%	2.00%
Segment Starting Value	$125,787	$113,031

THE SAFETY SEGMENT

At this point, you may well ask, "This all sounds great—but what if something happens outside of the plan? If our money's all locked into these segments, how can we afford to do things above and beyond that $7,000 or $10,000 a month, if we want? Where's that extra money going to come from, and what impact will it have on us long term if we spend it? And...what if we live beyond a thirty-year retirement?"

You do indeed want to make sure you have some money available outside of these segments if you want or need to make use of it. And yes, given the advancements in medical science and your healthy habits, you have a very good chance of living beyond your mid-nineties.

Where is that money?

If you add up all the investments in the model above, you will find that we've only used $1.265 million of your initial $2 million nest egg to invest in our six segments. That means you still have well over $700,000 to place in what I will call your Safety Segment.

These dollars will not be needed to provide your basic retirement income stream. We're going to keep this money out for "extras," and invest it carefully and safely to make sure you never have to touch your basic income-generating assets.

Even if you live really long lives.

The Safety Segment will give you both confidence and peace of mind. You will know that your whole portfolio has not been dedicated to your income stream—you have a safety net in place, invested for the long term because you won't need it all in the short term. If it lasts, you can also consider this Safety Segment as the money you may leave to your kids and grandkids as a legacy.

Of the $700,000 in our Safety Segment, we're going to keep $250,000 in liquid savings. I think it's important to keep a good chunk of your Safety Segment liquid, because I find that people make better overall decisions when they have sufficient liquidity.

You will panic less easily, and you will stay less emotional about downturns in the market when you have a quarter million dollars available in a simple savings account, not earmarked for anything specific.

A QUICK SUMMARY OF THE INCOME PLAN

So, Jack and Jane, let me just summarize the overall approach to make sure you understand what we're doing.

Together, we decided that you needed an average of $90,000 a year in today's dollars during your expected thirty-plus -year retirement. Some of that money is going to come from your Social Security incomes. And some will come from income generated by your nest egg.

You are going to use $1.265 million of that nest egg to be placed into six segmented investments, which will pay off in five-year increments over the next thirty years. With the remaining $700,000-plus, I'm going to create a Safety Segment, which can supplement that $90,000 a year, as needed, and also make sure you have some money to take you past thirty years, in case, God willing, you live very long lives.

To make this game plan work, you will have to do some budgeting. But mostly, you will need the fortitude and self-discipline to leave these segmented monies invested until their proper time. You will have to take the long view. And yes, that means resisting the urge to sell off during downturns, or to tap future money for use in an earlier year.

EVERY DOLLAR HAS A SPECIFIC JOB

Another way of looking at the self-discipline of the game plan is to remember the phrase:

Every dollar has a specific job. Never ask a dollar to perform a different job than it was assigned.

The dollars in the early segments have the job of providing you income in the early years of your retirement. The dollars in the later segments are there to grow and protect the later years of your retirement. If you owned a company with workers assigned to manufacturing, shipping, and plant maintenance, you would never ask a worker to do someone else's job. Or get distracted thinking about another goal than the goal you told him or her to achieve.

Think of your retirement dollars as your workers, and keep them focused on their assigned positions.

Or, like me, you can think about a basketball team, where the big guys score and rebound, and the little guys run the show. The team, as a whole, performs much better when everybody follows the game plan and does what they were assigned to do.

Here's the whole picture, with all the segments:

JACK AND JANE'S RETIREMENT INCOME PLAN

SEGMENT	1	2	3	4	5	6	SAFETY
Years	1-5	6-10	11-15	16-20	21-25	26-30	
Income Duration	5 Years	5 Years	5 years	5 Years	5 Years	5 Years	As needed
Income Start Year	1	6	11	16	21	26	As needed
Monthly Income in Today's Dollars	$8,333	$8,333	$7,500	$7,500	$7,000	$7,000	As needed
Inflation-Adjusted Income	$8,333	$9,660	$10,079	$11,685	$12,643	$14,656	Variable
Deferral Rate of Return	N/A	2.00%	3.00%	3.00%	6.00%	6.00%	Variable
Withdrawal Rate of Return	0.00%	2.00%	2.00%	2.00%	2.00%	2.00%	Variable
Segment Starting Value	$274,980	$285,241	$233,827	$243,081	$125,787	$113,031	$724,053

Total Social Security income: $45,000 per year, rising at 2% per year
Total initial investment in the six income-producing segments: $1,265,000
Total Safety Segment investment: $724,053
Total Spending for the Life of the Plan: $2,569,934

ANOTHER LOOK AT RISK

You can think about the six segments as a sequence of investments, but you can also think about them as a *sequence of risks.* Remember how the greatest timing risk comes at the very beginning of your retirement? If you lose money in the beginning, it can be almost impossible to make up those losses down the road.

That's why, in your case, we're *not taking any risk at all with your money during those first twenty years.* We'll place that cash in safe, fixed-income investments because we have to know that the money will be there when you need it. These Segment 1, 2, 3, and 4 investments might include CDs, municipal bonds, or fixed annuities, depending on the market and your particular circumstances.

As I said, I've assumed conservative rates of return. It's quite possible you could do better than 2% or 3% on these safe investments, but we can't be certain. At the moment, interest rates are extremely low, so we can be pretty sure they will be higher ten or fifteen years from now. You and I, however, will not count on that rise. In fact, as I noted earlier, we've actually assumed a 0% rate of return on your Segment 1 money—just to play it really safe.

In Segments 5 and 6, however, we will take some risk in the equities markets. We have to do that because we need to generate an average 6% rate of return while these funds are waiting to be used twenty-one to thirty years from now. We're taking risk, *but we're risking the very lowest sum of money:* a total of about $240,000 over Segments 5 and 6.

Emotionally, you will find it much easier to handle short-term losses on the stock market if you know your high-risk money doesn't have to pay off for twenty years or more. Thanks to the dedicated segments, you absolutely know that *you will not have to touch that money* in years one to twenty. Not only do you have your predictable income streams coming in through those first two decades, but you also have ample liquidity through your Safety Segment.

Your timing risk has been cut nearly to zero. So, when you tune into the media and the talking heads tell you the world is coming to an end, you can smile and say, "No, it's not. Not for me. If the markets crash, I can bide my time and wait for Segments 5 and 6 to recover and pay off. Let the storms blow."

What about that 81% probability of success suggested by the Monte Carlo trials? I can assure you that I have helped you increase that number. Not to 100%, but darn close. You can now sleep at night knowing you won't run out of money.

JACK AND JANE'S "PENSION"

"The goal of retirement is to live off your assets—not on them."

—FRANK EBERHART

So, Jack and Jane, now that you understand the model, I'd like you to take a couple of weeks before you sign up with my firm. At that time, we will invest your nest egg appropriately for each of the six income-generating segments, plus the Safety Segment.

Then we'll meet regularly to see if you're on track and make adjustments as needed.

For Segments 1 and 2, the money invested in short-term accounts, we will set up an electronic payment system to pay you your monthly income stream through direct deposits to your checking or savings account. You will get a monthly direct-deposit paycheck, just like when you were working, or just as if you had a reliable pension.

KNOWING WHAT'S "EXTRA"

You mentioned that you wanted to take your grandkids on some trips when they get a little older. Five years from now, when you hit seventy, your kids hit their mid-forties, and your grandkids get to Disneyland age, you can fly the whole brood to Orlando if you choose.

How can you do that without endangering your income stream? You go to your $700,000 Safety Segment and pull out $40,000 for a splurge. After all, the prime take-the-grandkids-to-Disney-World years come only once in a lifetime.

Never, ever, would you take $40,000 from Segments 1–6 for such a splurge. Forty thousand would be far too much money to remove from your income-generating funds. But with any luck, five years from now that $700,000 will be worth $750,000, and a $40,000 hit won't hurt a bit.

Crucially, with the Safety Segment, you have defined what's "extra," over and above your desired lifestyle needs. So, when you dip into that extra, you will do so with confidence.

Most people never make such a definition. Most people never know exactly what's "necessary" and what's "extra." And, as a result, many, many retirees can never splurge without fear.

THE KNOWING IS EVERYTHING

So, Jack and Jane—let's see how far we've come.

Before the game plan, you knew you had a nest egg of $2 million, but you had no clear idea how that nest egg would generate income to supplement your Social Security over a thirty-year time span.

You knew you had to take some risk in the markets, but you didn't know where, how, or when to take that risk.

You knew you needed a fund for "extras," but you had no idea how much of your money you could spare outside of your income-generating investments.

I'm hoping, dear Jack and Jane, that you now see a clear path into your future. I'm hoping you can visualize how *Your Retirement Game Plan* will work to provide security over the long haul.

You now know how much you can spend each month. You now know what constitutes a splurge. And you now know that your plan will likely work, no matter what happens in the markets or the economy.

In short, it's my fervent hope that I have lifted a whole load of fears and worries from your shoulders. It's my hope that you will enjoy every single day of your retirement, starting today.

CHAPTER 8

NAILING YOUR GOALS

The world is quite ruthless in selecting between the dream and the reality, even where we will not."

—CORMAC MCCARTHY

I look at a lot of people's retirement plans, often when they are referred to me by my current clients. These are usually friends who admire the way my clients have managed to retire successfully, and heard about my clients' more disciplined approach to investing. They come to my firm for an outside look at their own path.

In fact, so many people were asking us for a second opinion on their retirement plans that we started a formal "second opinion service." We will go through a discovery meeting with them to get very clear on where they are now, where they want to go, and what gaps may exist. Then we give these good folks an honest assessment of their situation.

Almost always, the discussion leads to one of three outcomes:

1. "Keep doing what you're doing, because you seem to be on a glide path to success. Your financial advisors are taking good care of you." We haven't gained a new client, but we've made someone happy. I see no reason to disrupt someone's investment portfolio and long-term retirement arc if they're already doing all the right things.
2. "We see some things you could improve, but we are just not the right fit for you." Why would we say something like that? Well, to be honest, sometimes people just don't have enough money to establish a long-term relationship with us. Or, they simply aren't looking for the kind of long-term planning my firm provides. We identify the weaknesses in their situation, offer some guidance, and then recommend them to a financial advisor better suited to their situation. I have to tell you, these folks really seem to appreciate our time and effort.
3. Or finally, we may say, "We can help you. We can make a difference and help you achieve all that is

> important to you and your family." Then we set up the investment plan meeting and put the wheels in motion to create their game plan. We are now well on our way to establishing a long-term relationship.

In all three outcomes, we have found our clients thrilled that we took the time to advise their family and friends. In a lot of cases, our clients are leaders in the community and pillars of their families, where they are looked up to by many. Because they've had some success, they find themselves routinely asked for investment and retirement planning advice—but they're not always comfortable dispensing it. Our second opinion service gives them another way to provide their friends and family members useful advice. Some become our clients, some do not; but they all receive attention to their individual situations.

ASKING YOURSELF THE RIGHT QUESTIONS

"I can't change the direction of the wind, but I can shift my sails to get where I'm going."

—JIMMY DEAN

Even if we can't help people with full-blown wealth management and game planning, we can often get them to focus on the right questions. We can help them stop asking themselves, "Do I have enough money to retire?" and start asking, “How much income will I need when I retire and where will it come from?” And, of course, “Am I accounting for the three great risks?”

Recently, a couple came to me to discuss their $1 million portfolio. They were friends of a good client, and I’ll call them Pete and Dawn.

Pete wanted to retire right away, but my client had urged him to ask me for a second opinion. The couple had worked out an entire retirement plan and a corresponding investment strategy with another firm—a firm that had told Pete to go ahead and retire.

Still, something didn’t feel quite right. Pete and Dawn worried that the other firm seemed to have rushed through the whole planning process. It had created a lot of charts and graphs, but all the documents seemed a bit “simplistic.”

“We’re just not feeling confident,” said Pete, “in spite of all *their* confidence.”

Pete was a successful consultant. Dawn had recently retired from the local school district. Together they had been earning well over $200,000 a year, and they wanted to have at least $10,000 a month coming in when Pete called it quits.

Dawn had a small pension of about $1,000 a month from her work with the schools, with only $900 a month in Social Security. Pete wouldn't be getting any pension, but his Social Security would be $2,500 a month—larger if he waited to retire and allowed it to accrue. Importantly, the two of them had a lot of demands on their money—the biggest being a $213,000 mortgage still outstanding on their house.

No situation is ever "simple," and always includes something unique. In Pete's case, he and his siblings jointly owned their mother's house. She was headed for a nursing home, so they were going to sell the house. Out of that sale, he would realize about $80,000, of which $60,000 would be dropped onto Pete and Dawn's mortgage. When this occurred, the couple would still have about $150,000 in outstanding debt.

As you have seen, timing can mean everything to a successful retirement. When I crunched the numbers, I saw that if Pete and his wife retired right away, they would face a large gap between what they could be *sure* to bring in and what they either needed or wanted. This would put a lot of stress on their portfolio in the early years.

But if they kept working, they should be able to pay off the mortgage in three-and-a-half to four years. At that point, the million dollars would have grown, as it would not have been eaten up by several years of retirement.

WAITING TO BEGIN SOCIAL SECURITY

Also, if Pete waited a little longer to tap his Social Security, it would grow up to 32% larger, rising to around $3,300 a month. As of this writing, people get an 8% increase in Social Security for each year they wait to begin, up to four years. At age seventy, Social Security no longer grows.

Just as importantly, Pete and Dawn needed to consider the spousal benefit in current law. When a person passes on, the surviving spouse then receives the larger of the two benefits for the rest of his or her life. In this case, if Pete predeceased Dawn, she would receive his larger $3,300 benefit, instead of her much smaller $900 one—to my mind, a critical piece of the puzzle.

Planning for the needs of a surviving spouse represents a vital aspect of my work—and it's statistically proven that there are far more widows than widowers.

At that point, I was almost certain Pete and Dawn's retirement game plan would be ready for the hardwood of the court.

LOOKING THE TRUTH IN THE EYE

We met again in my office a week later, and I said, "Four years from now, when you have successfully paid off your mortgage, you should be able to retire very comfortably. But you have to make the right decision on the front end, because it's really hard to change course later on. What happens if you realize that you retired too early and you have to start looking for a job seven or eight years from now?"

Like Bill from the oil company, who we met in the Introduction, Pete did not leave too happy after that visit to my office. As the truth sunk in, however, his outlook changed.

Although he is probably not thrilled to still have to get up on Monday mornings, Pete did call me back just the other day to say, "I really appreciate you taking the time to do what you did. It's not exactly what I wanted to hear, but I'm really glad you didn't sugarcoat the situation for me. I guess my wife and I knew all along that the numbers didn't really add up for me to retire right now."

I find Pete's response pretty common. I think many people know intuitively they can't really retire *just yet.* But they're hoping some financial advisor will pretty up the numbers and tell them otherwise. Unfortunately, we're always looking for the answers we want to hear.

What would I have done if Pete had decided to go ahead and retire anyway, and then had asked me to manage his million-dollar portfolio?

I would have respectfully declined. I simply would not have entered into a relationship that I knew had a high probability of a failing outcome.

BALANCING RISK

"If you do not change direction, you may end up where you are heading."

—LAO TZU

Without a well thought out game plan, it's easy to make mistakes on how much risk you take in your portfolio. Those mistakes can go either way.

I've had clients with plenty of money to create a secure retirement, but their investments were so aggressively placed that they were truly putting their financial futures in jeopardy. One bad market scenario and they could easily drop from a high probability of success to a low probability, indeed.

But I have to say that most people whose portfolios I evaluate are taking *too little risk.* As a result, they will likely never see a day when they can retire comfortably.

Both mistakes usually occur because people have no clear understanding of their overall financial situation. They have no plan that can tell them whether they're on the right track—or even where to find the right track.

I remember one woman who came to me—a good businesswoman with a successful company. She had all of her money in cash, and she said:

"I refuse to take *any* risk with *any* of my money. And I refuse to tie my money up because I may need it."

"Do you have any investments to fund your retirement?" I asked.

"No, because, like I said, I don't want to tie it up or take risk. I'll worry about retirement when the time comes."

"Uh, okay," I said. "I guess there's not much I can do for you, then."

With someone that close-minded, I see little point in launching a discussion of the greater risks of inflation, timing, and longevity. I say greater, *because the three great risks often outweigh the long-term risk of the market.*

But this woman simply would not accept such a truth. She has gaping holes in her roof and she refuses to let me help her fix them. I don't want to be held responsible when the inevitable storm comes. I really don't like to play in games where I can't possibly win.

FIVE SIMPLE GOALS VS. YOUR INSTINCTS

"We are not retreating—we are advancing in another direction."

—DOUGLAS MACARTHUR

We've talked about the proper mental attitude for any athlete or any investor: stick it out, play with a team, and accept the inevitable ups and downs the game will throw your way.

We've looked at the importance of planning around long-term risks. And we've learned how to use the market without emotion.

Now, by way of a summary, I want to bring together everything we've learned into five simple goals. Keep these goals front-of-mind, commit to *Your Retirement Game Plan,* and you will nail your best possible chance at retirement success:

1. Reduce the impact of your emotions.
2. Focus on growing your income.
3. Mitigate your three great risks: timing, inflation, and longevity.
4. Preserve your principal, especially early in retirement.
5. Invest over long periods of time.

Let's see how *Your Retirement Game Plan* directly supports these five goals. And, let's see how it will help you fight some basic human instincts to stick with those goals.

1. CONTROLLING YOUR EMOTIONS WITH THE GAME PLAN

I know I've said it again and again, but I cannot overemphasize how crucial it will be during your retirement to understand and gain control over your emotions. Once you stop drawing a paycheck and see your dependency on your investments, every downturn will seem like a catastrophe—unless you have a plan that gives you confidence and a reason to stick with that plan.

How does the game plan keep you calm?

Most people react with bad short-term emotional "instincts" to market upturns and downturns. Other people make money by feeding those instincts. But because you will have gone through a systematic consultative process, you will know you have accounted for *all* the issues in your retirement, and you will not panic.

Because the specific investment segments are directly targeted to specific five-year periods, your emotions should never be drawn into "all or nothing" investment impulses.

The liquidity provided by the Safety Segment will also help calm you down. With that liquidity, you will *know* you can likely bridge market downturns and the emotional crises provoked by the media.

If you have additionally chosen to hire a long-term wealth management company (see the next chapter), you will also have an on-court coach to keep those emotions under control.

As I said, follow the plan and you can ignore CNBC forever.

2. FOCUS ON A GROWING INCOME WITH THE GAME PLAN

Never forget that the word *growing* is just as important as the word *income.* Let me repeat that most clients who come to me say, "I have enough income," when they are only talking about "income for today." They will certainly need more tomorrow.

The long-term segment strategies in the game plan are created to provide an ever-increasing income over time.

3. MITIGATING THE THREE GREAT RISKS WITH THE GAME PLAN

We've discussed timing, inflation, and longevity in much detail. But let me just repeat how important it is for you to understand these risks, keep them forever in mind, and stick to the game plan to beat them.

Once again, human nature will work against you.

Only the rare individual grasps the full implications of financial timing, much less the timing of their own retirement and investments. By reading this book, you have been forearmed, but I would urge you to always crunch the timing numbers with a professional.

Only the rare individual really believes in inflation. It's strange, given the facts right in our faces. But humans have a tendency to live in the moment, and to imagine that things are going to stay pretty much the way they are. We know intellectually that everything, and especially prices, never stay the same for long. But we don't act like we know this truth. In the future, *things are going to cost more*; and, even without increasing your lifestyle, your costs will increase.

And finally, only the rare individual expects to live into his or her nineties, even though more and more do. Most people assume they will die much younger, but end up being wrong. How old did your parents grow to be?

The game plan actually looks out thirty-plus years and anticipates a long life.

4. PRESERVING YOUR PRINCIPAL WITH THE GAME PLAN

Without the seed corn, you will never realize the harvest. To make any game plan work, you must have principal to invest, and that principal must be protected early in the game. That's why, in our retirement income plan, we will likely use extremely conservative investment vehicles for the first four segments. Lose too much money in the early part of the game, and the second half of the game will likely be lost as well.

Because you have invested in carefully planned segments, you may also be protected from impulsive investments. Thanks to the segments, you may well remember that the *only* purpose of each chunk of money is to provide income for a specific five-year period of your future life. The segments may force you to recall that this money is not for taking a flier on a hot stock. It's not for dropping into an investment property in Hawaii. It's not for funding your son-in-law's hip restaurant idea. Done properly, the game plan will keep your "eyes on the prize."

5. INVESTING OVER LONG PERIODS OF TIME WITH THE GAME PLAN

You simply cannot succeed over a thirty-plus year time span without taking some risk. But, in our income plan, we will likely push most of the risk out past twenty years, where those who have invested in the stock market have been very successful.

By pushing out the market risk, and keeping short-term money safe, you will likely achieve several goals at the same time: quelling your emotions and overcoming the three great risks. Understanding, using, and controlling risk is the secret of truly "conservative" investing.

CONCLUSION

THE CEO'S SECRET

"A smart man makes a mistake, learns from it, and never makes that mistake again. But a wise man finds a smart man and learns from him on how to avoid the mistake altogether."

—ROY H. WILLIAMS

If you look at your personal finances—and especially your retirement finances—as a business, then you play the role of CEO, the chief executive officer of that business. There's no escaping your ultimate responsibility for yourself, your spouse, and perhaps several dependents. The buck does stop with you.

But any good CEO knows that the top job is too big to do alone. Any good CEO knows he or she must delegate effectively or their enterprise will be crippled by a single individual's lack of time and expertise.

The first and most important job to delegate must be the CFO. A good chief financial officer will take the burden of financial management off the shoulders of the CEO, and make sure the money's always there to make all the rest possible.

The same can be said of the family business called "retirement." This business has many aspects, from income flow to estate planning to charitable giving—the whole basket we call wealth management. Indeed, when you retire, sound financial management becomes more important than ever before in your life.

WHAT'S YOUR EXPERTISE?

"An investment in knowledge pays the best interest."

—BENJAMIN FRANKLIN

Do you have the expertise to play both CEO and CFO of your retirement? You may have been a terrific architect, doctor, inventor, salesperson, airline pilot, athlete, or even businessperson. But during your working life, your primary business focus was probably your work, not your personal finances. Did you develop the financial and investment skills necessary to create, execute, and monitor an effective game plan?

And, even if you do have those skills, you are on the verge of *retirement*. You're probably looking to spend less, not more, time crunching numbers. Less time talking to lawyers. Less time reading about the markets and meeting with accountants. I'm guessing you want to spend more time thinking about your travel plans, your grandkids' soccer games, and all the things you put off or missed when you were working full time.

IT'S ABOUT MORE THAN INVESTMENTS

One secret of a great CEO is that he or she has hired a great CFO to crunch the numbers, track the paperwork, and make sure all the legalities stay in place.

Every day, the subject of wealth management grows more and more complex. Laws change. Markets shift. It's really impossible for anyone but a full-time professional to keep up with all the issues, watch all the numbers, move the money when it needs to move, and bring the CEO the right advice at precisely the right moment.

In this last chapter, I want to urge you to hire a wealth manager whose number one priority is making sure that you can be a great CEO during your retirement. And I want you to remember that a good wealth manager will worry about a lot more than just your investments.

I can't tell you how many times I run into people who have solid investment plans in place, but fail to put together the proper legal and protective measures. They pay too much in taxes, and they leave themselves vulnerable to predators. You might have a million-dollar retirement plan today, but if you don't have the right insurance and you have a car accident in which you cause a serious injury, you will no longer have a retirement plan at all.

You may be healthy and fully in charge today, but if you become incapacitated without the right powers of attorney and healthcare directives in place, you may lose control of your own health and assets.

Do you need long-term care insurance? Do you have heirs who might need financial trustees to keep them on track? You may think you have provided for your heirs, but unless you keep your estate plan up to date, it may be irrelevant when it's needed by your loved ones. Lots of wealthy people die without proper wills and trusts, leaving a mess for their loved ones to sort out in court.

You may have an impressive IRA account today, but if you

are uninformed about the requirement of taking a series of distributions starting at age 70½, you will get hit with a 50% penalty. That's not later than April 1 in the year after you turn 70½. Not seventy and not seventy-one. Confusing? You bet. Do you need help keeping such dates and numbers straight? I'm guessing you do.

If you are uninformed about the benefits structure of Social Security, the consequences can be just as grave. For example, if you take your benefits starting at age sixty-two, the first date you can possibly take them, you could leave tens of thousands of dollars on the table.

You can spend the first years of your retirement becoming highly informed on all these issues, reading much longer books than this one, and setting up calendars and spreadsheets for your future self. And while you're getting informed, you can make catastrophic mistakes in the very earliest, most-crucial period of your retirement planning.

Or, like a good CEO, you can delegate.

Along with tracking dates and numbers, a good wealth manager will make sure the right professionals are brought in to keep everything up to date and buttoned down.

And of course, a good wealth manager, like a good coach,

will help you keep your emotions in check. Indeed, the biggest risk of "going it alone" is that no one will be there when you need to separate your misplaced instincts from facts and long-term plans. Many smart people make some really bad decisions when it comes to their own money.

A good wealth manager will slow you down, remind you of the five goals, and keep you on track.

TRUSTING THE POINT GUARD

"Winning isn't everything, it's the only thing."

—VINCE LOMBARDI

As this book comes to a close, I cannot help but take us back to the basketball court and return to the metaphor of the point guard.

When you hire a wealth manager, you are relying on him or her to help you make smart decisions with your money. You will be placing monies directly in the care of this person, and you will be depending on him or her to suggest timely adjustments that you need to make.

That means you must find someone with an established record of success. Someone many other people can vouch for. A proven professional with the right skillset to give you confidence and earn your trust.

That means you have to ask tough questions. Complete your due diligence. Call references.

You also need to find someone who, like a basketball point guard, will be your coach on the court—right out in the middle of the action. Someone who will go beyond "employee" and become an invaluable member of your team.

Find a good point guard and you will be halfway to a terrific retirement. Follow *Your Retirement Game Plan,* and you can sleep soundly each night, ready to wake with confidence for each morning of your next great adventure.

Here's wishing you a long and happy life, free from fear and blessed with countless joys.

—SAM MARRELLA

ABOUT THE AUTHOR

SAM MARRELLA began as a financial advisor with EF Hutton before moving on to Morgan Stanley Dean Witter, where he worked for fifteen years and rose to the position of Senior Vice President. In 2002, he joined Marrella Financial Group, the wealth management business founded by his father and brother. A self-described "people person," Sam is a CERTIFIED FINANCIAL PLANNER™ professional, a Retirement Income Certified Professional, and a Certified Planner in Long-Term Care who has dedicated his career to helping hundreds of clients achieve a comfortable and confident "life after work."

89633502R00104

Made in the USA
Columbia, SC
17 February 2018